The Watch House

Adapted by Chris Foxon
Based on the novel by Robert Westall

T0188676

LONDON · NEW YORK · OXFORD · NEW DELHI · SYDNEY

METHUEN DRAMA
Bloomsbury Publishing Plc
50 Bedford Square, London, WC1B 3DP, UK
1385 Broadway, New York, NY 10018, USA
29 Earlsfort Terrace, Dublin 2, Ireland

BLOOMSBURY, METHUEN DRAMA and the Methuen
Drama logo are trademarks of Bloomsbury Publishing Plc

First published in Great Britain 2023

A catalogue record for this book is available from the British Library.

A catalog record for this book is available from the Library of Congress.

ISBN: PB: 978-1-3504-5540-5
ePDF: 978-1-3504-5541-2
eBook: 978-1-3504-5542-9

Series: Modern Plays

Typeset by Mark Heslington Ltd, Scarborough, North Yorkshire

To find out more about our authors and books visit
www.bloomsbury.com and sign up for our newsletters.

Laurels and Papatango Theatre Company present

THE WORLD PREMIERE OF

The Watch House

Adapted by Chris Foxon

Based on the novel by Robert Westall

The Watch House is for a pair of Toms:

Thomas Edward Foxon (26 November 1916 – 30 March 2016), my grandfather.

And Thomas Albert Foxon (born 11 September 2023), my son.

The best of northern lads.

The Watch House

Adapted by Chris Foxon
Based on the novel by Robert Westall

Cast
in order of appearance

Geordie/Arthur	**Donald McBride**
Anne	**Aoife Kennan**
Fiona/Prudie/Da Souza/Timmo	**Catherine Dryden**

Director	**George Turvey**
Set & Costume Designer	**The Set Guise**
Lighting Designer	**Simon Cole**
Composer	**Beccy Owen**
Stage Manager	**Michael Byrne**
Assistant Stage Manager	**Mia Hartley-Oliver**
Consultant Stage Manager	**Julia Crammer**
Photography	**Topher McGrillis**
Press Representation	**Only In Newcastle**

The Watch House was first produced by Laurels and Papatango Theatre Company, 5–23 December 2023.

This playtext went to print before the production opened, so may differ slightly from the text in performance.

Donald McBride | Geordie/Arthur

Donald McBride trained at Hull University and Bretton Hall.

Theatre includes *A Nightingale Sang in Eldon Square*, *Tales from the Back Yard*, *The Last Post*, *Twelve Tales of Tyneside*, *Laughter When We're Dead*, *Oh! What a Lovely War*, *Close the Coalhouse Door*, *A Proper Job*, *Kiddars Luck*, *Come Snow Come Blow*, *In Blackberry Time* and *Green Fingers* (Live Theatre); *The Pitmen Painters* (Live Theatre/UK tour); *Romeo and Juliet*, *The Two Noble Kinsmen* and *A Midsummer Night's Dream* (Royal Shakespeare Company); *Keepers of the Flame* (Live Theatre/Royal Shakespeare Company); *A Nightingale Sang* (Octagon Theatre, Bolton); *Aladdin*, *Get off at Gateshead*, *Beamish Boy*, *Talkin' Heads* and *The Likely Lads* (Gala Theatre, Durham); *A Christmas Carol* (Northern Stage); *Beautiful Game* (Theatre Royal, Newcastle); and *Between Two Worlds*, *Pericles*, *Nothing Like the Wooden Horse*, *Bobby Robson Saved My Life*, *Dan Dare*, *Tom and Catherine*, *Cuddy's Miles*, *Sleeping Beauty*, *Mother Goose*, *Pickets and Pigs* and *Aladdin* (Customs House, South Shields), as well as productions for Nottingham Playhouse, Harrogate Theatre, Leeds Playhouse, Orchard Theatre and Theatre Royal Plymouth.

Film includes *Billy Elliot*, *Bliss*, *School for Seduction* and *The Old Oak*.

Television includes *Spender*, *Auf Wiedersehen Pet*, *Casualty*, *Byker Grove*, *The Bill*, *Harry*, *Crocodile Shoes*, *Emmerdale*, *The Tide of Life*, *George Gently* and *Danny and Mick*.

Radio includes extensive work for the BBC.

Aoife Kennan | Anne

Aoife Kennan trained at LAMDA.

Theatre includes *Scratches* (Arcola Theatre); *The 4th Country* (Park Theatre); and *For Services Rendered* (Jermyn Street Theatre).

Film includes *Blue Jean*.

Television includes *Vera*, *The Dumping Ground* and *Victoria*.

Aoife is also a writer. Her play *Scratches* premiered at VAULT Festival and was nominated for OffWestEnd and VAULT Festival Awards. She was one of the winners of the Sky Comedy Rep writing scheme in 2023.

Catherine Dryden | Fiona/Prudie/ Da Souza/Timmo

Catherine Dryden trained at RADA.

Theatre includes *The Pitmen Painters* (UK tour); *Mary Stuart* (Almeida Theatre); and *The Play That Goes Wrong* (UK tour/West End).

Film includes *Some Rules*, *Love in the Time of Coronavirus* and *Make My Boyfriend Better.*

Television includes *Vera* and *Traces*.

Radio includes *Homefront*.

Robert Westall | Author

Robert Westall made a sensational debut with *The Machine Gunners* in 1975. It won the Carnegie Medal and Westall established an international reputation. He won the Carnegie Medal for a second time in 1982 with *The Scarecrows*, becoming the first writer to win the award twice. He also won the Guardian Award in 1990 for *The Kingdom by the Sea* and a Smarties Prize in 1989 for *Blitzcat*. His books have been translated into many languages and dramatised for television. The story of his childhood is told in his autobiographical writings *The Making of Me*. He died in 1993 at the age of 63.

Chris Foxon | Adaptor

Chris Foxon studied at Oxford University and the Royal Central School of Speech & Drama. Since 2012 he has co-run the multi-award-winning Papatango Theatre Company. In 2022 he was named in *The Stage* 25 list of leading theatre-makers; in the same year Papatango won the Olivier Award for Outstanding Achievement in Affiliate Theatre.

As a writer, Chris was published in the 2023 Crossing the Tees short story anthology and is the co-author of the bestselling book *Being A Playwright: A Career Guide for Writers* (Nick Hern Books).

As a producer, Chris has staged acclaimed world premieres including: *Old Bridge*, winner of Olivier, Critics' Circle and two OffWestEnd Awards (Bush Theatre); *Some of Us Exist in the Future*, *The Silence and the Noise* and *Ghost Stories from an Old Country* (UK tour); *Shook* (Southwark Playhouse/UK tour; also broadcast on Sky Arts); *The Funeral Director* (Southwark Playhouse/UK tour); *Hanna* (Arcola Theatre/UK tour); *After Independence*, winner of the Alfred Fagon Audience Award (Arcola Theatre/BBC Radio 4); *The Transatlantic Commissions* (Old Vic Theatre); *Donkey Heart* (Old Red Lion Theatre/West End); *The Fear of Breathing* (Finborough Theatre/Akasaka Red Theatre, Tokyo); *The Keepers of Infinite Space* (Park Theatre); and *Happy New* (West End).

Chris has lectured at universities including Oxford and York. He is a trustee of November Club, a performing arts charity in Northumberland.

George Turvey | Director

George Turvey co-founded Papatango in 2007 and became its sole Artistic Director in January 2013. In 2022 he was awarded the Genesis Foundation Prize and was also named in *The Stage* 25.

As a dramaturg, he has led the development of all of Papatango's productions, including the Olivier Award-winning *Old Bridge*. Direction for Papatango includes: *Here* (Southwark Playhouse, nominated for three OffWestEnd Awards); *The Silence and the Noise* (UK tour); *Shook* (Southwark Playhouse/UK tour, nominated for seven OffWestEnd Awards including Best Director and Best Production; also broadcast on Sky Arts); *Hanna* (Arcola Theatre/UK tour); *The Annihilation of Jessie Leadbeater* (ALRA); *After Independence*, winner of the Alfred Fagon Audience Award (Arcola Theatre/BBC Radio 4); *Leopoldville* (Tristan Bates Theatre); and *Angel* (Pleasance London/Tristan Bates Theatre).

George trained as a director on the National Theatre Studio Directors' course and as an actor at the Academy of Live and Recorded Arts (ALRA). He has appeared on stage and screen throughout the UK and internationally, including the lead roles in the world premiere of Arthur Miller's *No Villain* (Old Red Lion Theatre/West End) and *Batman Live* World Arena Tour. He is the co-author of *Being a Playwright: A Career Guide for Writers*.

The Set Guise | Set & Costume Designer

The Set Guise are a set building company based in the North East of England, working in theatre, events, film and television. Their clients include the BBC, Northern Stage, Live Theatre and Sam Fender.

Simon Cole | Lighting Designer

Simon Cole is a lighting and projection designer from the Tees Valley. He works across multiple art forms, from intimate theatre projects to contemporary art installations and large-scale outdoor events. He has also worked as a technical and production manager for companies across the UK. He is an associate artist of Curious Monkey Theatre.

Theatre includes *Penguin* (Curious Monkey Theatre); *Tiny Fragments of Beautiful Light* and *All White Everything But Me* (Alphabetti Theatre); *Worlds Apart* (Woven Nest Theatre); and *Skybound* (TimbaDash Theatre).

Beccy Owen | Composer

Beccy Owen is a musician, singer, songwriter, performer, producer, musical director and sound designer with over 25 years of experience. Her work has historically focused on the human voice, using rich harmony, playful vocal techniques and mesmeric rhythms to place audiences at the heart of a singular musical experience. Her awards include the Special Recognition Award at the Journal Culture Awards.

Theatre includes *Mother Courage and Her Children* (Albion Electric Warehouse, Leeds); *Lands of Glass* (Summerhall, Edinburgh); and *The Amplified Sanctum* (The Glasshouse).

Supporters

Many thanks to Arts Council England, Backstage Trust and the Mouth of the Tyne Collective, whose support made *The Watch House* possible, and to November Club for supporting the position of stage manager with a training bursary as part of their GROW programme.

"Remarkable unearthers of new talent." *Evening Standard*

Papatango is an Olivier Award-winning theatre company. In 2022 our leadership team was named in *The Stage* 25, a select list of theatre-makers shaping the industry's future.

We provide pathways into theatre, especially playwriting, for artists and audiences otherwise without access to professional resources. All our opportunities are free, assessed anonymously and open to everyone.

Our flagship programme is the Papatango New Writing Prize, the UK's first annual award to guarantee a new playwright a production, publication, royalties and commission, as well as to offer commissions and showcase readings to its shortlist. All entrants receive feedback on their scripts, an unmatched commitment to supporting playwrights. 1,553 entries were received in 2022, meaning the Prize attracts more annual submissions than any other UK playwriting award – yet is unique in giving support to all. Prize-winners have transferred worldwide, earned many awards and risen to the forefront of theatre.

Papatango also run a Resident Playwright scheme, taking a new playwright through commissioning, development and production. Residents have toured the UK and transitioned to full-time creative careers.

Writers launched by Papatango have won BAFTA, Olivier, Critics' Circle, *The Times* Breakthrough, OffWestEnd, RNT Foundation Playwright and Alfred Fagon Awards, and premiered internationally and in the West End.

We use their astonishing success to inspire others. Our GoWrite programme delivers free playwriting opportunities nationwide. Young people in state schools, SEND centres, pupil referral units or charities supporting mental health or other bespoke needs write plays which are professionally performed and published. Our Young Playwrights Award and Summer School produce talented young writers on major platforms, with professional collaborations and mentoring. Adults join workshops or courses at a variety of regional venues culminating in free public performances, and can access seed funding to support their own productions.

We thus deliver free face-to-face training for over 3000 writers, producers and makers each year, with travel bursaries to ensure anyone can join us.

Our motto is simple: all you need is a story.

"Every year Papatango comes up with a bit of a cracker."
The Guardian

For up-to-date news and opportunities please visit:

www.facebook.com/pages/PapaTango-Theatre-Company/257825071298

www.twitter.com/PapaTangoTC

www.instagram.com/papatangotc/

www.papatango.co.uk

Artistic Director George Turvey

Executive Director Chris Foxon

Creative Learning Producer Sarah Emily Parkes

Funding and Development Manager Ruth Tosha Mulandi

Resident Playwrights

May Sumbwanyambe
Samantha Potter
Sam Grabiner

Dare Aiyegbayo
David Lane

Board

Stephanie Bain (Chair)
Serena Basra
Sally Cookson
Sam Donovan

Davina Moss
Nicholas Rogers
Tom Wright

Papatango Theatre Company Ltd is a registered charity and a company limited by guarantee.

Registered in England and Wales no. 07365398.
Registered Charity no. 1152789

Housed in a 125-year-old social club in Whitley Bay, Laurels is the only producing house in the whole of North Tyneside.

Founded by Olivier Award-winning theatre-maker Jamie Eastlake and comedian Steve Robertson, the 3,500 square feet "Adult Byker Grove" is a warren of rooms housing three bars, events spaces, offices and a full-time small-scale professional theatre.

With its year-round theatre and comedy programme, artist development and a whole host of projects on the slate for stage and screen, Laurels has become a force to be reckoned with in the North East scene since opening in the summer of 2021.

Standout productions such as *Gerry & Sewell: A Purely Belter Adventure*, *The Club: A CIU Story* and *Juggling* have cemented the theatre as a place for lower socio-economic voices, telling stories for the region from people rarely represented in an industry in which they are seldom heard.

www.laurelswhitley.co.uk

Chief Executive & Artistic Director Jamie Eastlake
Head of Comedy Steve Robertson
Projects Producer John Hickman
Events Manager Jade Young

Acknowledgements

First and foremost, thanks to the Robert Westall Estate for trusting me to adapt his cracking ghost story for the stage.

I am profoundly grateful to Jamie Eastlake and the team at Laurels for being so supportive, opening their precious Christmas slot up to a project I pitched them out of the blue. Laurels is a vital asset to Tyneside, taking bold risks on new artists and new stories and keeping our culture alive.

I am even more indebted to my good colleagues and better friends at Papatango, George Turvey and Sarah Parkes, whose warm encouragement, astute notes and willingness to cover some of my day-to-day work while I wrote made *The Watch House* possible. In particular, George has been an absolute rock, as he has for so many early-stage writers. I have always known he's brilliant at his job, but now I've experienced that first-hand.

Many thanks also belong to the November Club team, for their staunch commitment to developing new talent in Northumberland and the imaginative and impactful way they achieve this.

To our creatives and cast: you're all geet big heroes.

All of the support I've been so fortunate to receive would have been for nothing without my wife, Hannah Jenner. In a year in which we got married, moved house and had a baby, she agreed I could add to the madness by writing a play too, then threw herself into somehow making it all work. How joyful, dauntless and above all selfless: typical Hannah, in other words. I am very lucky (as is our beautiful son Tom, who already knows his mum is the best person in the world).

Hannah, Tom and I have only managed to stay afloat through all of this because of the love and kindness of our family and friends. Thanks to Val and Nigel Foxon, Janet Jenner, Alan and Jacky Jenner, and the rest of you. Yes, even the ones who dragged us into the freezing North Sea on our wedding day (happily, the services of Tynemouth Volunteer Life Brigade weren't required).

On that note, the final and most important acknowledgement must go to the extraordinary people who have run Tynemouth Volunteer Life Brigade for almost two centuries, saving countless lives. For anyone interested, the breeches buoy Arthur describes to Anne was last used in 2005 – but whether through that or more modern methods, the

Brigade rescues hundreds of people every year, being called out in the most dangerous conditions imaginable. These volunteers represent the best of the seafaring tradition which defines Tyneside. Please visit the Watch House or otherwise support their work. The final words must belong to them:

Tynemouth Volunteer Life Brigade

On the afternoon of 24 November 1864 a fierce south-easterly storm sprang up. Two ships, the schooner *Friendship* and the passenger steamer *Stanley*, were wrecked on the notorious Black Middens on the north bank of the Tyne. Several attempts were made to aid the stricken vessels but even though thirty-two people were saved, by the following morning another thirty-four had lost their lives: twenty-one passengers and five crew from the *Stanley*, six crew from the *Friendship* and two lifeboat men. This all happened within yards of thousands of spectators lining the cliff tops. There was a huge public outcry over the loss of life.

One of the spectators was Captain John Morrison, a volunteer at Tynemouth Castle. He suggested to John Foster Spence and his brother Joseph, both aldermen of the town, that if a body of men were formed to aid the Coastguard, then possibly more lives could be saved. They wrote a set of rules, had them agreed by the Board of Trade (who looked after the coast at that time) and a public meeting was arranged for 5 December 1864, with free tobacco to encourage volunteers to sign up. Over 140 men did. On that evening T.V.L.B. was formed.

The Board of Trade circulated the rules around the coast with a strong suggestion that this was a 'Good Idea'. Eventually almost every village on the coast had a Volunteer Life Saving Company. These companies eventually became the Coastguard Rescue Service of today. T.V.L.B., however, remained independent, and is now a stand-alone declared facility to HM Coastguard, doing the same job as an HM Coastguard team and using the same equipment and procedures, enabling us to work closely with the flank Coastguard teams.

The Watch House

Characters

Geordie, *male, seventies, our narrator. For most of the time he's on stage, he only talks to us, unseen by the other characters – until he is. He and Arthur are to be played by the same actor; the audience might not realise they're separate characters until Act Two.*

Anne, *female, mid-teens. A girl transplanted from North London to North Tyneside.*

Arthur, *male, seventies. A retired fisherman, he now looks after the Watch House.*

Prudie, *female, seventies. Arthur's sister, she lives with him in a cottage by the Watch House.*

Timmo, *any gender, late teens. A sixth-form student. Written as male in this script, in keeping with the original novel, but name and/ or pronouns can be altered.*

Father Da Souza, *male, late thirties or early forties. A Roman Catholic priest. American.*

Fiona, *female, early forties. Anne's mother.*

Other roles to be played by members of the company as needed.

Note on Casting

This play can be performed with a cast ranging in size from three to six.

Suggested doubling for a cast of three is:

Geordie/Arthur (always to be played by the same actor, regardless of cast size)

Anne

Father Da Souza/Timmo/Prudie/Fiona

Clearly, gender and age don't need to be represented literally. This is, after all, a play about ghosts.

But get the Geordie accents right. Now that does matter.

Setting

The play is set in North Tyneside – specifically, the coastal stretch from Longsands Beach to North Shields Fish Quay via Tynemouth Castle and Priory, a couple of miles of beautiful beaches, ancient sites and proud people. At the heart of it all, perched on a hill where the river meets the sea, is Tynemouth Volunteer Life Brigade. Also known as the Watch House, it is the place where today's Coastguard service began. A sprawling wooden building, with a low rectangular main body and a couple of viewing towers, it is painted white; the interior is now a museum, bursting with maritime artefacts, paintings of the coast, old uniforms, etc.

The play unfolds in 1979.

The action takes place over a couple of weeks, to fit into the window of any school holiday – pick whichever most closely coincides with the dates of production. Costumes and music, especially at the disco in Scene Six, should reflect whether it's Christmas, Easter or summer.

Production Notes

This script calls for a lot of flickering lights. Of course, if you find alternative ways to stage it, that's fine. But as written, a warning for anyone with light sensitivities would be sensible.

Scene ends can be marked with blackouts and exits, or kept fluid with characters remaining on stage – whatever works best.

Act One

Scene One: The Arrival

Geordie   I watched them come sweeping along Front Street, grand as you like in that fancy Rolls. Course, they took the turn by the Clock Tower too fast, course they bloody did. They went down that hill like they were dropping anchor. Brakes shrilling like a gull begging some of the morning catch. I tell you, their faces were white by the time they climbed up the other side and pulled in at the Watch House. Right pair of wallies.

Mind you, the girl's not so bad. Poor bairn grew up in London, but she can't help that. Now she's here, she'll soon learn. I'll see to that.

No, it's her ma who's to blame. Miss Fiona what was born and bred here, she should know better than to barrel along like that. Mind, it's been that long since she bothered visiting, it's no wonder she's forgot how to act. Forgot a few other things and all I bet, else she'd never leave her daughter at the Watch House. No, if she remembered, she'd keep her bairn far away. A million miles away.

But here they are. Waltzing right up to the cottage by the Watch House as if they owned it. Bloody fools.

Anne *and* **Fiona** *enter. They don't see* **Geordie**. *No one except the audience does. For now.*

Fiona *rings the bell of the cottage.*

Fiona   God, this place hasn't changed one bit. I thought they'd have eradicated that fishy smell by now.

Anne   Yeah, so dumb of them to put a Life Brigade by the sea.

Fiona   Be as snarky as you like with me, young lady, but just you wait and see how Prudie and Arthur take to your lip. Spending the holidays here will do you the world of good.

Fiona *rings again.*

Anne   I'll miss you too, Mother, but we must try to be strong.

Fiona *glares at her, defeated, and jabs the bell even more urgently.*

Fiona   Come on, come on!

Geordie *becomes* **Arthur**. *The audience should assume that he's always been* **Arthur**, *that it was* **Arthur** *addressing us earlier, that it was* **Arthur** *who watched the women drive up. He comes up from behind them, to* **Fiona***'s surprise.*

Arthur   A'reet?

Fiona   Christ, Arthur! Must you creep up like that?

Arthur   Sorry you didn't have a clear enough view from the top of this ruddy great hill, pet. It's hard to see anything coming, that must be why they went and built a Watch House on it.

Anne   I think my lip's going to do just fine here, Mother.

Fiona *glares at both of them, unlikely allies.*

Fiona   Anne, this is Arthur, Prudie's brother. Since you're already such fast friends, I'm sure he'll show you round. Not that there's much to see, is there, Arthur?

She laughs. **Arthur** *and* **Anne** *don't.*

Fiona   I was expecting Prudie to meet us. Has she been detained?

Arthur   Eh?

Fiona   Is. She. Somewhere. Else?

Arthur   No. She's. Not. (*Relenting.*) She'll be in the kitchen, cooking up a storm for both of yis. Won't have heard the bell.

Fiona   I'll have to miss her. I simply must get back to London.

Anne   Just say hello to Prudie. She's been cooking especially.

Arthur *catches the vulnerability.* **Fiona** *doesn't.*

Fiona   Eat it on my behalf. You'll have no trouble with that, will you?

Arthur (*protesting*)   There's nobbut a scrap of meat on the lass! (*More gently.*) It would do you both good to stay for some proper scran. And Prudie would hold it a great favour to see you again, Miss Fiona.

Fiona   No, Arthur, I must be off. But give her my regards. My most cordial regards, of course.

Anne   Mum, please.

Fiona   Don't be such a baby, Anne. I'll sort everything out with your father, then before you know it I'll be back to pick you up. Be good.

Anne   Mum –

Fiona   Toodles!

She leaves, perhaps giving **Anne** *a quick pat, perhaps not.* **Arthur** *and* **Anne** *are alone.*

Pause.

Arthur   I've not seen you since you were a babby. Course, you won't remember.

Anne   No.

Arthur   Your da came up an' all. Nice feller. How is he?

Anne   OK.

Arthur   I was sorry to hear about the divorce, like.

Anne   OK.

Pause.

Arthur   Well, let's show you what's what.

Anne *moves towards the cottage.*

Arthur   Where the bloody hell are you off to?

Anne   You were going to show me round . . .

Arthur   Aye, the important stuff. Not the cottage, we just live there. No, you need to see this.

His expansive sweep takes in the land, the sea and, most of all, the Watch House.

Anne   Do I?

Arthur (*ignoring her*)   Tynemouth, lass. Where the greatest river in the world meets the greatest sea. Over there, them ruins, the Castle and Priory. Them knights and monks watched over this place for centuries. Once they were gone, it was our turn. The fisherfolk built this Watch House, right where we're standing, over a hundred year ago.

Anne   It's a bit nippy –

Arthur   Mind you, its proper name is the Life Brigade. But we call it the Watch House, cos that's what it does. Watches over us. It was the first coastguard.

Anne   Fascinating.

Arthur   Isn't it just. Built cos of them rocks at the river mouth, see? Sharp, hungry little buggers. Called the Black Middens, cos the Midden Man used to dump all the nightsoil from the Tynemouth netties there, for the tide to wash away.

Anne   Gross.

Arthur   The name's right, cos those rocks turned many a fine ship into nowt more than rubbish.

Anne   They don't look like much to me.

Arthur Oh aye? How'd you feel after a thirty-foot wave lifted you sky high and you come smashing down on them, like a coconut on a spike? One south-east gale, we lost twenty-seven fishing-smacks in a single day. All the men drowned in sight of their own homes, their wives and bairns looking on from the cliffs.

Anne (*interested in spite of herself*)   That's sad.

Arthur Sad? It's bloody tragic, that's what it is. That's why they built the Watch House, so if ever a ship were in trouble, the alarm would sound and a rescue be launched.

Anne And that's what you do?

Arthur *laughs, a little sadly.*

Arthur Nah, them days is gone. Long gone. When they built the twin breakwaters – see? One here, at North Shields, one there at South Shields – they robbed the Black Middens of their danger. The river's as tame as a kitten now. And the Watch House is just a bit o' history.

Beat.

That's what me and Prudie do. Live in the cottage, make sure the old place divvent fall apart, and tell anyone who cares to listen what the Brigade once was.

Anne I didn't have much choice but to listen.

Arthur Suit yourself.

He turns away.

Anne No, wait. Sorry.

Arthur *shrugs. The jury's still out.*

Anne I'm just a bit . . .

Pause. He takes pity.

Arthur Divvent fret, hinny. It's not easy for any o' us.

Anne Honestly, I did like hearing about the Watch House.

Arthur   So did your ma, back when Prudie was her nanny. Then she outgrew us.

Anne   Now she's outgrown me too.

Arthur   Aye, well . . . Once you're unpacked, I'll take you round the Watch House. But you look half-frozen, me yapping on, and Prudie will bloody murder me if I keep you from her any longer. Come on, into the cottage.

They enter the cottage. This is **Prudie**'s *domain – neat, comfortable and, above all, clean.*

Arthur   Prudie! The bairn's here.

Prudie *bustles in, eager – though a little deflated when she sees that* **Anne** *is on her own.*

Prudie   Miss Anne! I never heard the bell.

She gives **Anne** *a hug.*

Prudie   But where's your ma?

Anne *looks awkward.* **Arthur** *takes over.*

Arthur   She couldn't stay, pet. She was gutted, but the motorway's clogged up and she was worried about being caught in the dark.

Prudie   Oh.

Arthur   She sent you her love, like. All her love.

Anne *looks at* **Arthur**, *grateful.*

Prudie   She always was a lamb. Well, I'll just have to make do with you, Miss Anne, won't I? Let me look at you.

Anne, *unsure what is required, gives a little shuffle, half bow, half jig. It's ridiculous but seems to satisfy* **Prudie**.

Prudie   Oh, I haven't seen you since you were a babby.

Anne   Arthur said.

Prudie   Did he now? But I bet he didn't say you're all skin and bone. You need a good scran.

Anne   Actually he did.

Prudie   Then that's the first sense that man's shown all day. Do you know, Miss Anne, this morning he traipsed in here with a bag of fish and dumped it all over me table.

Arthur   Nowt wrong with fresh fish, straight from the quay. Best way to be paid for a job of work and all, better than a ten pound note. Not even the bloody Tories can take your fish off you.

Prudie   I wish they would. I've been scrubbing the smell out all day. I bet Miss Fiona noticed, delicate nose she's got. Did she, Miss Anne, did she notice the smell?

Anne (*awkwardly, not wanting to get* **Arthur** *in trouble*)   Well, maybe a little.

Prudie   I knew it! You stupid man, slopping fish scales all over me linen, purple guts sliding everywhere. I tell you, Miss Anne, I found a long white spine, sticky gobbets all over it, right where you're standing. Gobbets, right there.

Anne *looks peaky.*

Prudie   Here's some more! (*She dives down and comes up with a handful of gunk, which she waves at* **Arthur**.) All that's to say you need feeding up, Miss Anne, put some flesh on you. I've fishcakes, and lovely wobbly jelly for afters.

Prudie *says all this while waving the fish goo under* **Anne**'s *nose.* **Anne** *retches.*

Prudie   None of that, now. You'll eat it all, like a good lass. I'll be watching.

She marches **Anne** *out to the kitchen, ignoring her pleas, leaving* **Arthur** *alone on stage. He becomes* **Geordie** *again, though the audience won't realise that just yet.*

Geordie   It's been a good while since we had a bairn at the Watch House.

Beat.

You might think this place is all hunky-dory. It looks reet enough, I grant you, all clean and bright. But that's just whitewash. Scrape beneath the paint and you'll find agony, layer on layer of agony, as old as the timbers. You'll find *him*.

Scene Two: Out And About

It's the next morning – day two – in the cottage. **Prudie** *is bustling about.* **Anne** *enters.*

Prudie   Did you sleep well, Miss Anne?

Anne   I guess. In between you checking on me at midnight, 5 a.m. and 8 a.m.

Prudie   You don't need as much sleep when you're older, so I'm glad I could be there each time to help you nod off.

Anne *rubs her eyes tiredly.* **Arthur** *enters.*

Arthur   Morning, hinny. Coming into toon?

Anne   Newcastle?

Arthur   Divvent be daft, man. What's Newcastle got that Tynemouth hasn't? I mean Front Street. Got errands to run.

Prudie   Yes you do, Arthur Herbert McGill, and you idling the morning away in that damn Watch House of yours.

Arthur   I was waitin' for the bairn!

Prudie   Waitin' for your behind to grow another inch, more like. Get on with you.

She exits.

Anne   Have you and Prudie always lived together?

Arthur   Aye, ever since me mam brought her into the world via our front parlour.

Anne   That must be why you get on so well.

Arthur *snorts.*

Arthur   I wouldn't trade my sister for all the fish in the sea, but that divvent mean I divvent yearn to throttle her five times a day. That's just family, isn't it?

Anne   I suppose.

Arthur   But she's a reet jewel, Prudie, deep down. Besides, families stick together.

Anne   Do they?

Pause. **Arthur** *has put his foot in it.*

Arthur   Come on. I'll introduce you to me best pal.

He points out the window to his pony. They leave with the pony.

He's a surly, mad-eyed beast, he is, but at my age, this hill's a bit tough on the knees. So me old Gallower pulls the cart. You best walk beside us, pet, your knees being just dandy. He won't be happy to pull you and all. He's a bit of a tricky bugger, but once you get used to his ways you'll be fine.

Anne *reaches out to pet the pony. She jerks back as he lunges.*

Arthur   He likes a finger, so he does. Got a taste for them when he lived by the primary school.

Anne   I'll keep an eye out for kids with four fingers. Where are you going?

Arthur   Post office, for me pension. Bugger there is scared of the pony, so I always ride right up to him. Mind you, he's not used to livin' somewhere civilised. Come up from London, only been here twenty year.

Anne   I've only been here one day.

Arthur   Aye. But you're not doing too bad for all that.

Pause.

Look, you divvent want to hang about wi' me all day. I'll crack on, you go and explore the castle or summat. There are some brilliant tombs. Get to know the place. Make friends.

Anne   In a graveyard?

Arthur   Best kind of friend. Never answers back, always there when you need them.

Anne   You'd hope so!

Arthur   Most of my mates are in there now. Off you gan, pet.

He and the pony pass on towards town, leaving **Anne** *to enter the grounds of Tynemouth Castle and Priory. Crumbling walls and myriad leaning old gravestones, on a wind-battered headland jutting into the sea. We hear the gulls and the waves.*

Anne (*wandering and reading tomb inscriptions*)   'Ernest "Ernie" Fenwick. 1792–1814. Beneath the waves, dark and deep, he found eternal sleep; none remain to weep.' Jesus.

Da Souza *enters, unseen by* **Anne**.

Anne   'Verity Barlow. 1806–1864. We all have a debt to nature due; she paid hers and so must you.' Thanks for those inspiring words, Verity.

'Joseph Armstrong. 1785–1839.'

Da Souza (*interrupting, to quote the inscription*)   'He was a fine baker, but for all his famed pies, never again to have a good rise, unless it's to meet his maker.'

Anne   Oh. You heard me?

Da Souza   Don't worry. I often talk to myself too.

Anne   I wasn't talking to myself.

Da Souza   Is that so much worse than talking to dead people?

Anne   I wasn't doing that either! I was *reading*.

Da Souza   I wouldn't recommend that. (*Fingers his dog collar.*) Reading's what got me into this mess.

Anne   You're a priest?

Da Souza   For my sins.

He offers his hand.

Father Da Souza.

Anne *shakes his hand.*

Anne   Anne.

Da Souza   Just Anne?

Anne   Melton. For now.

Da Souza   You look a mite young to be getting married.

Anne   My mother wants to go back to being McGuire. And she says I have to as well.

Da Souza   Ah. Your mother, is she local? I don't know a Mrs Melton. Or a Miss McGuire.

Anne   She was, but she's been in London twenty years.

Da Souza   And you've run away to join the navy?

Anne   She's dumped me with Arthur and Prudie at Watch House Cottage while she sorts the divorce. Prudie used to be her nanny. I think she's the only friend Mum's got left.

Da Souza   There are worse places to be dumped, Anne.

Anne *shrugs.*

Da Souza   Believe me – I speak as an upstanding American, plucked to do missionary work in the most savage places of the Earth. Have you seen Sunderland?

Beat.

Do you know anyone else here? Besides Joseph the unrisen baker.

Anne   No.

Da Souza   Splendid! Well, not splendid, but it means you'll be free on Saturday evening?

Anne (*warily*)   Maybe.

Da Souza   Then you must come to a disco a friend of mine is throwing. Father Fletcher. He runs a youth club. C of E, so it will be very dull, but all the better for you being with us.

Anne   Thanks. But I don't –

Da Souza   You said yourself you were free.

Anne   It's not really my thing.

Da Souza   At least think about it. It will beat being alone at the Watch House.

Anne   You know the Watch House?

Da Souza   Yes, I do. About as suitable a place for a young lady as this miserable graveyard.

Anne (*defensive*)   I like it. Arthur's going to show me round, tell me about its past.

Da Souza   Is he now?

He looks like he will say more, but they're interrupted by a howl. It's not unearthly – just a dog – but should still provoke a shiver.

Anne   What was that?

Da Souza   Well, a dog?

Anne   Thanks, Reverend. I meant, where did it come from?

She heads off towards the howl. **Da Souza** *reluctantly follows.*

Anne   These graves have been pawed at.

Da Souza   You know, Christians and wild beasts don't have a happy history. I'm not ready to become a saint.

Anne   It's dug at more graves here too. Yet others haven't been touched.

Da Souza   An inferior vintage?

Anne   Look!

The dog enters. It's a mangy creature, not much threat but still uncanny in its wretchedness.

Poor thing. It's half-starved.

Da Souza   Certainly hungry enough to nibble at a nice plump priest. Leave it be, Anne.

The dog whines. **Anne** *reaches out, coaxingly. The dog whines again. Then, suddenly, it lunges.* **Da Souza** *pulls her back just in time. He falls over, shouting in panic:*

Jesus Christ!

And the dog scarpers.

Anne (*shakily*)   Isn't that blasphemy?

Da Souza   Certainly not. Exorcisms are always most effective from a horizontal position.

He picks himself up gingerly, dusting off bits of mud.

That's my story, and I'm sticking to it.

He toes the edge of one of the graves.

I should let Father Fletcher know his parishioners are no longer resting in peace. He might want to book a rabies shot before he tries to re-inter them.

Anne   That's the second animal which has tried to bite me today. I must be cursed.

Da Souza   Talking of feral beasts with a taste for human flesh, are you sure I can't tempt you to that disco?

They grin at each other.

Scene Three: The Watch House

The next day – **Anne**'s *third in Tynemouth.*

Geordie *is in the Watch House. As before, the audience should assume this is* **Arthur**.

He watches **Anne** *pick her way through the artefacts. She lifts some up, runs her fingers over others, looks puzzled at everything. She still can't hear or see him.*

Geordie   Finally! Anne's traipsed all over bloody Tynemouth before finding time to visit us at the Watch House. Young lasses these days divvent know a good time when it presents itself.

Anne *peers, disturbed, at an old skull.*

Geordie   That's one of our treasures, that is. Dredged up from the Black Middens. Go on, give it a shake, girl.

Anne *recoils in disgust.* **Geordie** *tuts. She moves on to examine other objects.* **Geordie** *is our guide, following her around.*

Geordie   Them name plates were retrieved from ships lost on the Middens. *HMS Iron Crown. The Cactus*, out o' Blyth she was, cracking little ship. My favourite's the *City of Bristol*, cos of the naked lasses. Bristols from Bristol, eh? Nymphs, some posh bloke called 'em once. I said to him, you call them what you like, mate, I know what they are and you know what they are and we aren't looking at them for the name are we? He went all red.

Ah, now them two big tin cans, they saved a man's life. Captain of the *Jurneeks* of Riga jumped overboard holding 'em, one under each arm, and floated all the way to shore. I'd like to see Heinz manage that.

Them figureheads also come from wrecks. Give me the shivers, like. Whitewashed, eyeless. That mermaid's missing her heed. That general's split from his neck to his bal . . . crotch. So many ruined bodies. Every splinter an agony.

Anne *picks up a plaque.* **Geordie** *flinches.*

Geordie   Leave that be!

She puts it down. He watches, still tense.

Anne *finishes her investigation.*

Anne   Arthur! Are you there?

Geordie *becomes* **Arthur**.

Arthur   Aye, pet.

Anne   What's this?

Arthur   Ah, that's me pride and joy. I made it.

Anne (*uncertainly*)   It's very nice. What is it?

Arthur   Breeches buoy, to rescue ships in trouble on the Middens. I made the model to show visitors. See? Here's the ship. And here, coming doon from the cliffs: three hawsers. Ropes to you, lass.

He picks up an Action Man. As he talks, he mimes firing a rocket with gusto, travelling back and forth on ropes, etc.

The men from the Brigade would fire a geet big firework, taking the hawsers to the ship. Then, fixed up good and proper, you'd run a breeches buoy, a big sort o' basket, to the ship and back to shore, getting everyone off safe. See – Action Man, though I call him Aqua Man, me little joke, he's getting to and from the wreck, safe as houses.

Anne   Wouldn't they just use a helicopter now?

Arthur (*dejected*)   Aye, they bloody would. Not that it matters any more. Since they built them breakwaters, the waves is tamed. No need for any rescue on the Middens, breeches buoy or helichopper.

Anne   Helicopter.

Arthur   That's what I said. Here, have a gander at this other model. St Mary's Lighthouse, just up the coast, Whitley Bay. More like Shitley Bay. But the Lighthouse is all right.

Anne   It's beautiful.

Arthur   She lights up an' all. Flick the switch.

Anne *does. The lights flicker on and off* (*even if we can't see the model itself*).

Anne   It even turns like a lighthouse. That's brilliant, Arthur.

Arthur (*embarrassed*)   Ah, I divvent know about that, pet, but I'm pleased with it. Go on, best turn it off now, the wiring goes haywire if you leave it too long.

Anne *turns it off. The lights stop.*

Anne   Why is all this stuff here, Arthur? All these . . . souvenirs?

Arthur   I s'pose there wasn't no other place to put what come from the wrecks. It wouldn't be right to throw them out. The Watch House is somewhere to keep them, to . . .

Anne   Commemorate them?

Arthur   Aye. It's where poor drowned folks are remembered.

Anne   It's like a shrine to the sea's dead. I'm not sure I like it so much now.

Arthur   Ah, well. One last thing, then we best be getting in for tea or Prudie will be on the warpath. This is a painting of *The Hoplite*. She come aground in 1854. All the way from Australia, only to be scuppered by rocks outside her home. Bloody tragic. Lots of them bones come from her.

Anne   Why aren't they buried in the Priory?

Arthur   Never had the names to go with them, and no one come to claim them, so they just got left. Reckon they're as peaceful here as anywhere.

Pause.

I'll nip and get the kettle on. You lock up.

*He passes **Anne** the keys and leaves.*

She's alone. It should feel and sound colder, creepier and darker.

Suddenly the lights from the model lighthouse start to flicker. She jumps.

Anne   Bloody wiring.

She heads back and presses the switch until the lights stop. She turns towards the door.

The lights come on again, flickering, if anything more insistent and more harsh than before.

For God's sake.

She returns to the switch and presses it. Nothing changes; the lights flicker even faster. Exasperated, she pulls the plug out and they stop.

There.

*She's almost at the door when the lights flicker on again, even though the plug's out. **Anne** turns, fearful. She stares, then runs for the door and exits.*

The lights flicker even more intensely, with a sinister build-up of sound.

Scene Four: The Message

*We're back in the cottage, the next morning – day four. **Prudie** is holding forth to **Arthur** and **Anne**. She thrusts a variety of foodstuffs under **Anne**'s nose – fruit, crisps, quiche, etc. **Anne** waves each away, only to be harassed with another. Ideally they'll get more elaborate as we go, perhaps culminating in an entire wedding cake or something equally absurd.*

Prudie   Your so-called handiwork will be the death of the bairn. Those bloody lights scared her out of her wits!

Arthur   It's just a loose connection.

Prudie   You've got a loose connection! You'll burn your precious Watch House to the ground with all your tom-fool electrics, and us in our beds with it.

Arthur   Our beds? Our beds aren't in the bloody Watch House, woman. Our beds are here!

Prudie   My brother, the prince of reason! First thing you do today, you go straight over there and you disconnect everything. Everything!

Anne   But I did unplug them, Prudie. They carried on.

Prudie   There, pet. I know you think you did, but you must have got the wrong plug.

Anne   Maybe . . .

Prudie   That's right. It was just an accident.

Anne   An accident.

Prudie   Because someone's too cack-handed to wire a plug properly.

Arthur   I'll check it all. Every last bloody bulb. All right?

Prudie   You better. Poor bairn's lost her appetite. Hasn't touched a morsel.

She regards the mound of food items sadly.

Anne   Can I go with you, Arthur?

Prudie   Back there!

Arthur   Course you can. Welcome in the Watch House whenever you like.

Prudie   What a pair! Why don't you go and make some friends, Miss Anne, folks your own age, rather than hanging around here petrifying yourself?

Anne   But I like being here, Prudie.

Prudie   Do you? When you've lived with that Watch House your entire life, with every man around you yapping on about it all day every day, you might feel different.

Beat.

All right, if you must.

She exits.

Arthur   Come on hinny, into the Watch House before she changes her mind.

They leave the cottage and enter the Watch House.

Anne   It's your safe haven, this place, isn't it?

Arthur   Aye. It was founded by Quakers, you know. Men of faith. They'd no truck with drinking or smoking or any kind of sin.

Anne   So that's why you find peace here.

Arthur (*with fervent devotion*)   Every time lass, every time.

He pulls out a bottle from a hiding place. **Anne** *is shocked.*

Arthur   The sailors knew how to hide the good stuff from them Quakers. I give thanks whenever I need a tipple Prudie won't learn about.

He takes a swig.

Anne   Arthur!

Arthur   Sorry, pet. Ladies first.

He offers her the bottle. She sniffs and recoils.

Me home brew's a bit of an acquired taste. Look, here's summat you will like.

He digs an old brass badge from his pocket and passes it to her.

It's one of the first Brigade badges – 1864. Anyone wearing that's a true man of the Brigade.

Anne   Or woman.

Arthur   Aye, or woman.

Anne *makes to pass the badge back.* **Arthur** *shakes his head.*

Arthur   No, lass, you hang onto it. Reminder this is your home.

Anne   Thank you. That's – thank you.

Arthur (*gruffly*)   You're welcome. Here, come up the tower, didn't show you upstairs.

They climb the tower.

This is where the Brigade watches for ships in distress. Best view in all o' North Shields. Just a shame it's of South Shields.

Anne   What's wrong with South Shields?

Arthur   You've heard of the north–south divide?

Anne   Yes.

Arthur   Well, it's a common misbelief that's about North England and South England. But actually it's about us in North Shields and them buggers in South Shields.

Anne   Right . . . Arthur, what's this?

Arthur   Searchlight. Off a World War Two cruiser. Scoot round and I'll signal to that ship.

He fiddles with it and a blaze of light shoots out. He pulls a lever and it vanishes, then reappears. Vanishes, then reappears.

Anne   What are you saying?

Arthur   Just telling him to steer clear of South Shields.

A return signal comes through.

Anne   What's he saying?

Arthur   'Bloody sand-dancers.' Got his heed screwed on, that one. Here, you have a look.

Anne *moves to his spot and looks out.*

Arthur   You see the shutters? That lever controls them, so you cut the light off and bring it back. Long or short, Morse code. Vital that every man jack o' the Brigade knew his Morse code.

Anne   I can see a figure too . . .

Arthur   There's a mirror above the shutters. It'll be your reflection.

Anne   But it doesn't look like me.

Arthur   I think that every morning. Get up, scrape a razor over this old face, wonder where the real Arthur went.

Anne *changes her angle, bends her head, testing the reflection.*

Anne   It isn't moving like me. It's . . . it's watching me.

Arthur   You're just not used to it. Dazzled by the light. I'll turn it off.

He does. The searchlight cuts out.

Anyway, chores to be done.

He heads downstairs. **Anne** *lingers, unsure.*

Arthur   Come on!

She follows him. Now they're together, downstairs.

Right. Everything's off at the mains, so no lights to make you jump. Got it?

Anne   Got it.

Arthur   Grand. Now to earn your keep. Prudie might not let you lift a finger in the cottage, but the Watch House is my domain. And she's dusty.

Anne   Oh no.

Arthur   Oh yes.

He whips a duster out of his pocket with a flourish.

The cabinets, them shelves, even the bones. You called it a shrine, so make it as clean as one.

He hands her the duster.

I'll be in the back room, doing paperwork. Important paperwork. Not to be disturbed.

Anne   I saw a bed in there.

Arthur   Never you mind how I does me paperwork. Now, get cracking.

He exits. **Anne** *begins dusting, unenthusiastically.*

Anne   Urg.

She stretches to dust the top of a cabinet and finds a pair of pants. She drops them in disgust.

That gives the Watch House a new meaning. Pervs.

She carries on. **Geordie** *enters. As before, the audience may assume this is* **Arthur***, talking directly to us – though this time, they might start to wonder . . . He watches* **Anne***, then speaks.*

Geordie   It's good to have young blood in this old place. You can feel its spirits lift.

Anne *reaches the bones. She picks up a skull and dusts underneath.*

Geordie   The drowned dead crumbling away to nowt. This is the first bit o' care they've been shown since they were lifted from the sea and brung here. Small wonder they respond.

Anne *stops dead in her tracks. She peers closely beneath the skull she's holding. Her lips move. She's deciphering something scrawled in the dust.*

Anne   What . . .? I wish Arthur hadn't turned the lights off, I can't see a damn thing.

She peers closer. **Geordie** *peers with her, reading alongside. She still can't see or hear him.*

Anne   A . . . N . . . H . . .

Perhaps at this point a light box or projection shows the writing. Perhaps not. Either way, the writing is shaky, clearly rushed and unsure, and should be read aloud as such.

E? E. L. And that's . . .

Geordie   P.

Anne   A. N. H. E. L. P.

Geordie   Anne. Help.

Anne   Anne. Help. Oh God.

The lights come on again, flickering as intensely as before.

Geordie   Anne! Help!

The lights flicker madly. **Anne** *exits in a panic.* **Geordie** *makes one final, whispered plea.*

Anne. Help.

Scene Five: The Old Feller

Once again we're back at the cottage, later that day. **Prudie** *is now accompanied by an entire buffet trolley of food. She stands, fierce, before a cowed* **Arthur** *and a shaken* **Anne**.

Prudie   I forbid it. No, Arthur, I forbid it. She's not to set foot inside that Watch House again.

Arthur   She's just letting her imagination run away with her.

Anne   I am not! And I can speak for myself.

She opens her mouth to do just that, but **Prudie** *takes the opportunity to stuff a pie into it.* **Anne** *chokes and subsides.*

Prudie   That place is off limits. Do yis hear me? Why, Miss Fiona would have a fit if she knew what was going on.

Arthur   Would she now?

Prudie   Don't take that tone with me, Arthur Herbert McGill. The bairn's my responsibility. You're not to go filling her heed with your nonsense.

Anne (*spitting out the food*)   I want to know what's going on!

Arthur   There's a legend about the Watch House . . .

Prudie   Arthur!

Arthur   She has a right to know, woman!

Anne   Yes!

Prudie   It's just hogwash. Old wives' tales. Nowt and less than nowt.

Anne   Then it can't hurt.

Arthur   Prudie. Better she hears it from me than some dimwit at Tynemouth market goes spouting in her lughole. Then she'll know it isn't no more than a story.

Prudie   You just want to sound off, like the old foghorn you are.

Arthur   She isn't the first to imagine things at the Watch House, and she won't be the last. It's easy to get all het up there, but nowt ever comes of it. Knowing that will do her good.

Prudie   Oh, very well. But Miss Anne, you're not to believe a word. Promise me?

Anne   How can I promise not to believe it when I haven't heard it . . .

She sees **Prudie**'s *face.*

Anne   OK, OK, I promise. Please, Arthur. What's going on?

Arthur, *enjoying the limelight, takes his time. Fills a pipe, cricks his neck, etc. Finally:*

Arthur   The Watch House is made o' wood, right? Old timbers stretched tight, sagging and creaking after years and years. Well, there's noises. Groans and whatnot.

Anne   That's not what's happening!

Arthur   All right, hold your horses. Not just noises. When a storm hits, the whole cliff shakes. Things shift about. Then after the planks dry and shrink, stuff on the edges falls with a geet big thump.

Anne   But –

Arthur *overrides her objection.*

Arthur   Whenever stuff like that happens, iffy electrics, kids writing silly messages in the dust, all o' it, we say it's The Old Feller. Or, The Old Feller's up to his tricks again. It was being said even before I joined the Brigade.

Anne   A ghost?

Arthur   It's just a joke that's lasted seventy-odd years.

Anne   So The Old Feller's not real?

Arthur   Oh, he was real enough. A little old man who gave his whole life to the Brigade. One of the first volunteers. Canny bloke, proper canny. He never missed a call whenever a ship was in distress.

Anne   Never?

Arthur   Never. His life's work. But then the doctor said he had a dodgy ticker and no more going out on the breeches buoy. Had to keep his feet dry. Even then, he haunted the Watch House, doing whatever he could. Painting walls, waving a collecting tin. Until . . .

Arthur *breaks off, a little sadly.*

Anne Yes?

Arthur Well, there was a big wreck. Fierce storm. Every man needed out at sea, but they rescued everyone. Only to find, when they come back to the Watch House, that The Old Feller was lying there, flat on his back, stone deed. He'd answered his last call.

Beat.

Not a bad way to go. I wouldn't mind it.

Prudie Sounds good to me. That would stop you filling the bairn's heed with guff.

Arthur Just telling you how the story goes.

Prudie The Old Feller's just an excuse for why you don't keep that Watch House tidy.

Arthur Aye, all right.

Anne But what was his name?

Arthur I divvent rightly know. I only heard the men talk about him as The Old Feller.

Anne That's so sad. To be forgotten.

Arthur He's not forgotten. What's important, lass: what you're called, or what you do? We still remember everything The Old Feller did for the Brigade. Rescued dozens, maybe hundreds. He was a hero.

Anne But that's not right. He was a person, a living, breathing person who stood right here. He deserves a name.

Arthur So you're not mad at him for scaring you half to death?

Prudie Arthur!

Anne It's OK, Prudie. Now that I've heard about him, I don't think he'd harm a fly.

Prudie The Old Feller isn't still around, pet! You need to get that straight.

Anne (*quickly, to spare* **Arthur** *more blame*)   I know. I just like hearing the history, Prudie.

Prudie (*mollified*)   All right, then. Now, I best be getting the tea on. You finish up these last few bits, Miss Anne, then we'll have some proper scran.

Anne *stares nervously at the buffet table. As* **Prudie** *bustles out,* **Arthur** *winks at her.*

Arthur   So you aren't put off the Watch House?

Anne   No. Now I'm used to it, I won't be caught out any more.

Arthur   That's the ticket. Nowt there to bother anyone sensible. I've been in and out of the place all me life and never had so much as a peep from The Old Feller.

He rises.

I'm going to smoke me pipe, before Prudie pressgangs me into laying that table. You do that, hinny, will you?

Anne   Of course.

Arthur   Good lass.

He leaves.

Anne *is alone. She brings out the Brigade badge, and traces it with her fingers.*

Anne (*whispers*)   Anne, help . . . I will. One member of the Brigade to another, I promise.

Scene Six: The Disco

The next evening. **Anne**'s *been in Tynemouth for five days.*

We're in a draughty church hall. Pop music plays from tinny speakers. **Da Souza** *is setting up a row of knock-off soda cans (the more bizarre or obviously ripped off from recognisable brands, the better). Every now and then he gives a cringe-worthy wiggle to the music.*

Anne *enters. She watches him, looking about nervously.*

Da Souza *starts to lip sync. He finally swings round, mid-pose, and sees* **Anne.** *Stops dead. They're both mortified.*

Da Souza   Anne.

Anne   Hi?

Da Souza   Hi.

Beat.

I do a mean ABBA, too, you know. It's not all hymns and carols.

Anne   I can see.

Da Souza   Yes, well . . . I wasn't sure you'd come.

Anne   Prudie was keen. She doesn't think I should be spending so much time with her and Arthur. When I said you'd invited me, she went, 'Oh, you must go, you must, even if he's . . .'

Da Souza   . . . 'a dirty RC who'll burn in hell'. Yes, thank you.

Anne   She didn't say that. Well, not those words. Or not all of them. At least, not in that exact order.

Da Souza   Clearly I'm growing on the locals.

Pause.

Anne   Is anyone else here?

Da Souza   Not yet. Not even Father Fletcher, whose idea this entire shebang was but who suddenly came down with a severe case of 'thought-better-of-it-and-scarpered'. So I was left to step in.

Anne   Or twirl in.

Da Souza   Hah. Yes.

Awkward pause.

I'm expecting the entire teenage population of Tynemouth to show up soon. Cut some shapes.

The music stops with a dying crackle. Depressing silence.

I'll see what's wrong. You, erm, have a drink.

He hands her a can. She takes it, dubiously.

He exits. **Anne** *is alone.*

Da Souza (*offstage*)   By the power of Christ, I compel thee.

The music starts up, then fades out with another sad crackle.

(*Still offstage.*) Damn.

Anne (*reading the can*)   'Poopsi'?

She takes a sip. It's rank.

Jesus!

Timmo *enters as she says this.*

Timmo   You've come to the right place for him. Is he answering?

Anne   No. Hello.

Timmo   Hello. Greetings. Salutations.

Pause.

You new?

Anne   Yes.

Timmo   Good. That's good. Not that you're new. Or not new. I don't care about that. No, what's good is that I was right. I observed you in the spirit of scientific enquiry, I discerned through a careful process of elimination of all the faces of all the girls I know that you hadn't been here before, and ineluctably I reached the devastatingly insightful conclusion that you must be new. At least, that is, new to Tynemouth. And new to the ways of Father Fletcher. I knew you must be new, you see, because if you weren't new to here, and to him, then you'd know not to bother coming here. Because I'm not new, I knew that. But because you are new, of all the things you knew tonight, not to come here wasn't one of them. So you did. But now you do know that, so you're no longer new. Or not so new as you were. Do you see?

Anne *stares at him, befuddled, unsure if he's taking the piss.*

Anne   I . . . I think so.

Timmo   I knew it. I'm Timmo, new girl. Timmo Jones. Progeny of the local sawbones, renowned scientist in my own right. Have a paw.

He offers his hand. Still a bit confused, **Anne** *shakes it.*

Anne   Anne.

Timmo   Just Anne? Mononyms aren't fashionable here, you know, despite the endless playing of Cher.

Anne   Oh God, I hope not . . . I'm Anne Melton.

The music finally starts again. It's Sonny and Cher's 'I Got You Babe'.

Timmo   Did I not predict it? Nonetheless, Anne Melton, let's dance!

Timmo *doesn't wait for her but leaps into the most wildly exuberant dancing, totally disregarding the rhythm of the music.*

If the size of the ensemble allows, others drift in and join the dancing, all more normal than **Timmo**. *Otherwise, he dances alone. Either way,* **Anne** *watches, left out.*

Timmo, *exhausted and sweaty, works his way back to her.*

Timmo   So, Anne Melton, why did you come here?

Seeing she doesn't know how to answer, he continues.

Let me enlighten you as to why I, a keen student of science, elevated above the mere frolics of mankind and possessed of the knowledge that Father Fletcher's discos are always dreadful, came. It is because they are so dreadful that only the lonely, the mad or the dangerous can be found here. All the things that make human beings interesting. Father Fletcher, sadly, is only lonely, which makes him only a third interesting. Which are you, Anne Melton?

Anne *stares at him, perplexed, unsure how to answer. He dances even more wildly.*

Secretive, eh? Go on, then, Anne Melton, tell me a secret which interests me.

Anne   . . . My parents are getting divorced?

Timmo   That makes you lonely. First of the three down. What else?

Anne (*starting to enjoy opening up*)   I live with two pensioners in a cottage by the Watch House. They're teaching me to rescue people from the sea with an Action Man.

Timmo   Excellent! The maddest thing I've heard all week. Second down. Anything else?

Anne   I . . . I think a ghost is talking to me through the lights in the Watch House!

The music should cut out just as she shouts that last line, so it echoes around the hall.

Timmo   And that ticks the dangerous box. Three out of three! Very well done, Anne Melton. You *interest* me. Come on, let's get out of here before Father Fletcher inflicts more of his Koala Cola on us.

Anne   It isn't Father Fletcher tonight. It's his friend, Father Da Souza.

Timmo (*admiringly*)   Anne Melton! The new girl knew something after all. Now tell me about these diverging parents, these aquatic pensioners and, most of all, this luminous ghost.

He pulls her away, towards the Watch House.

Scene Seven: The Skull

A few minutes later. **Anne** *and* **Timmo** *have slipped into the Watch House with a torch. They whisper.*

Anne   Welcome to the Watch House.

Timmo   I wish you'd let me turn the lights on.

Anne   Trust me, they're best left alone. And we don't want anyone to know we've snuck in. It's lucky you had your torch.

Timmo   I bring illumination wheresoever I tread. And in that spirit, I shall dispel all the superstitious piffle you've swallowed. I'll fix the wiring in the morning – I made Dad buy me a soldering kit for Christmas. He wanted to get me boxing gloves but I pointed out I could do far more damage to my enemies with molten metal.

Anne   Because that's normal.

Timmo   But first, tonight, I shall prove that there's nothing more sinister in this Watch House than asbestos. The Old Feller shall be exorcised before your very eyes.

Anne   You don't lack confidence, Timmo Jones, I'll say that for you. But you don't know the Watch House like I do.

Timmo   There I concede. I shall build my case, inexorable logical step by inexorable logical step. It shall be a priori beside the Priory!

Anne   What?

Timmo   A priori. Deductive reasoning.

Anne   Look, before you go off on one, let me make my case. The Old Feller's case. This is his house.

Timmo   All right.

Anne   First, we need to find out why a ghost needs help from the living.

Timmo   Problematic assumption one: that the message in the dust was meant for you. Problematic assumption two: that The Old Feller wrote it. Oh yes, and a tiny last one: that ghosts exist!

Anne   If I were Arthur, I'd 'bray' you.

Timmo   If you were Arthur, I wouldn't have followed you into a dark room.

Anne   All I'm saying is we need to learn who The Old Feller is.

Timmo   Further flawed reasoning. One –

Anne   One: shut up! Two: shut up! And three: shut up! We'll start with the photos. The Old Feller helped found the Brigade, so he must be in some.

Timmo   At last, a reasonable supposition.

Anne   Look for someone small. Any age, because he was young when he joined the Brigade and he stayed all his life, but small.

Beat.

And, I don't know why, but someone sad.

Timmo   Sad?

Anne   Yes. I just feel . . . he's sad. He asked for my help, after all.

Timmo   So you say.

They peer at the paintings and photos.

This one?

Anne   No, he's too jolly. He's joking with the guy next to him.

They look some more. It's a painstaking process, which allows time to think.

So, which are you?

Timmo   What?

Anne   Your three criteria for what make people interesting. Lonely, mad or dangerous. Which are you?

Timmo *creates a distraction.*

Timmo   What about him? No, hang on, he's sitting down but has long legs.

Anne   I think you're lonely. And just pretending to be mad.

Timmo   As long as you're terrified of how dangerous I am, that'll do.

They smile at each other.

More searching.

Anne   Here!

Timmo   Keep your voice down! You'll wake Arthur.

Anne   He's hunched. Standing apart. He looks so . . . forlorn. Haunted.

Timmo   Is that proof?

Anne   I know it. I can feel it. Him.

Timmo   Anne Melton, I shall now introduce you to scientific method.

Anne   Just bring that torch closer.

She leans in to study the photo.

Trevor Armstrong . . . Jonas Cuthbert Smith . . . Here! (*She breathes the name.*) Henry Cookson. That's him. The Old Feller is Henry Cookson.

She looks around the Watch House.

Hello, Henry Cookson.

Pause.

Nothing happens. **Timmo** *breaks the silence with a hoot.*

Timmo   Congratulations. You've found the ugliest specimen in all of the photos, so malodorous no one will stand near him, and decided he'll be your new boyfriend.

Anne   You sound jealous.

Timmo   I wouldn't call Henry The Old Feller. I'd call him The B.O. Feller.

A sudden piercing smash. They whip round.

What was that?

Anne (*shaky*)   This.

She holds up a skull – not the one she was admiring yesterday, but a different, darker, bigger one. It shines malevolently in the torchlight.

Timmo   It must have fallen. Smashed the glass.

Anne   Timmo . . . The skull was in the case. Something threw it from inside . . .

Lights come on in the cottage.

Timmo   Leave it, Anne.

She lays the skull down. They exit in a hurry, crunching through shattered glass.

Geordie *enters – though the audience may think it's* **Arthur***, they may also start to suspect the truth. Because it's* **Geordie***, he doesn't (can't) turn the Watch House lights on; he's lit only by those from the cottage. He stays well away from the skull.*

Geordie   It's you, isn't it? It's time you left this place alone. Let us be. Please, let us be.

Scene Eight: The Sea

It's the next morning: bright, birdsong, total contrast to the last scene.

Anne *and* **Timmo** *are on the Black Middens.* **Geordie** *is watching them.*

Anne's *pottering among the rocks, humming music from the disco.*
Timmo *wields a magnifying glass.*

Anne   That skull came from the Middens. There must be some clue about it in these rocks.

Timmo   It looked ancient. Anything's probably been washed away ages ago.

Anne   Are you always this grumpy after a late night?

Timmo *sticks a flamboyant finger up at her. She laughs and moves away over the rocks.*

Geordie   She's a canny lass, this one. Got up this morning, barely a wink of sleep, and just flew down the hill from the Watch House like an arrow, onto the rocks and into the tide. Glorious, to be young. I saw a lot here meself when I was a nipper. Aye, I saw a lot.

Anne *has found something in a rock pool.*

Anne   Timmo!

Timmo   It's just a rockpool. Unless this dead crab is the evil genius we seek?

Anne   A bone! It's all white and mouldy.

Geordie   Oh dear.

Timmo   Anne. I know London is landlocked, but surely you've seen seaweed before?

Anne   What?

Timmo   That's seaweed. A thick strand of knotted wrack. It must have split off from the bunch.

Anne   Knotted wrack?

Timmo   Ascophyllum nodosum. This is when you make an impressed noise.

Geordie *does make an impressed noise, though* **Timmo** *can't hear it.*

Timmo   I'm wasted on this crowd.

Anne   But it looks like a bone . . .

Timmo   Not really. You just want to find something. Confirmation bias.

Anne   I'm not biased!

Timmo   Of course you are. We all are. Any scientific study has to recognise and mitigate that. You're looking to confirm that The Old Feller exists, and that for some reason he goes throwing his skull around. You interpret what you find accordingly. To mitigate that bias, we have a devastatingly handsome and brilliantly analytical young man –

Anne   One more word and there will actually be bones in this pool.

Timmo   I heed your warning.

They continue looking.

Geordie   They're ignoring all them beautiful mussels. Go lovely in the pot, they would. Criminal.

Anne *hesitates, then speaks.*

Anne   I got a letter from Mum this morning. Well, Prudie got a letter.

Timmo   What news?

Anne   The lawyers are arguing over custody. Over me.

Timmo   That's their job.

Anne   But you know what, she barely mentions me. Just hoped I was behaving myself.

Timmo   Mere hours after you broke into the Watch House and caused untold damage.

Anne   I didn't cause anything! The Old Feller did.

Beat.

Mum wouldn't care even if Prudie caught us then wrote and told her. Waste of a stamp.

Timmo   Right.

Anne   I bet she doesn't even want custody. I bet the lawyers are only arguing over which of them has to take me.

Timmo   Hmm.

Anne   What?

Timmo   Isn't 'hmm' enough?

Anne   You think I'm not being fair to my mother? You don't know her.

Timmo   No, I don't.

Anne   But . . .

Timmo *turns away to peer at something with the magnifying glass.*

Anne   Go on.

Timmo   Look, I merely observe. And what I've observed is: One: your mother's had to move out, not your dad, yet it was all on her to find you somewhere to stay. Two: the only friends she can turn to are hundreds of miles away. And three: she's the only one writing to anyone. You aren't writing to her. And I've not noticed anything in the mail from your dad.

Anne   He doesn't care either.

Timmo   It can't be easy.

Anne   And I'm not worth the effort.

Timmo   That's not what I'm saying.

Anne   Isn't it?

Timmo   All I'm saying is your mum's got to be pretty lonely.

Anne   And you feel sorry for her because of her uncaring daughter?

Timmo   No –

Anne   I suppose you want a medal for Most Compassionate Twat of the Year?

Timmo   Look, I know what it's like to be alone, all right. I just think you might give her more of a chance.

Anne   You've deduced all this in the twenty-four hours you've known me.

Timmo   Actually it's . . . sixteen hours and thirty-eight minutes.

Anne   Oh, just . . . bugger off!

She storms away, over the rocks.

Geordie   She's close now. That's the spot.

Anne *suddenly comes to a standstill. Her body stiffens.*

Timmo   Anne? Are you OK?

Anne   I see a ship.

Timmo   What? Anne, stop messing around. I'm sorry, all right.

Anne *is staring straight ahead. She doesn't see him. She speaks tonelessly, as if reciting.*

Anne   I see a ship, full rigged, by the ragged traces of a blue moon. Aground on the rocks, its sails tattered, splitting. Desperate people crowd the sides, penned by the waves.

Timmo   Anne!

He shakes her. She pays him no heed. **Geordie** *has been watching closely.*

Geordie   She sees a host of men on the clifftop, fighting the wind and the rain. She sees them curse against the cruel sky. She sees them try three times to fire the breeches buoy. She sees them fail twice, but on the third, they land their mark.

Anne   I see a troop of women, hardened by a lifetime of toil on this rocky coast, come to the aid of strangers on a dying ship. I see them bend their backs to the ropes, hauling them tight. I see one man shed his oilskins and grip the rope, ready to descend into the storm.

Geordie   She sees one man shin along those ropes, back and forth, ferrying an entire shipload of people to safety, soul by soul, braving death again and again.

Anne   I see one man.

Geordie   She sees one man.

Anne *and* **Geordie** (*together*)   I see/She sees Henry Cookson, The Old Feller.

Timmo   Anne!

She comes to and sags, exhausted. He helps her from the rocks.
Geordie *is greatly moved.*

Timmo   Are you all right?

Anne   I . . . I think so.

Timmo   It was like you entered a trance.

Anne   I saw him. I saw The Old Feller.

Timmo   I believe you. Whatever just happened, I believe you.

Anne   He rescued people. He'd never harm us. Never.

Geordie *makes as if to comfort her, but can't.*

Timmo   So what does it mean?

Anne   It means there's something else at the Watch House.

Scene Nine: The Other

An hour later. **Anne** *is in the cottage. She's packing a rucksack with paranormal investigative items: torch, note pad, Bible, etc.*

Prudie *enters.*

Prudie   Miss Anne, whatever are you up to?

Anne   I've got some work in the Watch House.

Prudie   But Arthur's on his errands.

Anne   I know. This is my own . . . project.

Prudie   I won't have you setting foot in that place on your tod. Not after all the fandango.

Anne   Fandango?

Prudie   Rusty messages and flaming lighthouses.

Anne   That's not –

Prudie *takes the rucksack from her.*

Prudie   You'll content yourself with the cottage today, pet. Don't look like that! There's plenty of fun to be had with me. Here's an idea: we could plan the menu for the WI meeting!

Anne   Please no.

Prudie   Well, write to your ma. She's overdue a letter.

She sweeps out with the rucksack. **Anne** *unenthusiastically sits down to start writing.*

Anne   Dear mother . . .

She tuts and crosses it out.

Dear Mum . . . No.

More crossing out.

Da Souza *enters.*

Anne   Dear Fiona . . . Obviously not.

Another strike of the pen.

Dear Mother – oh, this is impossible!

Da Souza   How about 'Hi'? As my hip young friends would say.

Anne   'Hi.' OK, yes. Now to figure out the rest.

Da Souza   Alas, there I cannot assist you. No Roman Catholic priest has ever known what one woman says to another. Indeed, many of us have never known one woman.

Anne   Thanks for the start, anyway. Why are you here?

Da Souza   Prudie let me in, once she'd frisked me for relics, made sure I'm not converting you with a glimpse of St Ignatius's remarkably long and very crusty toe nails.

Anne   Do you actually keep dead people's toe nails?

Da Souza   Don't pull that face. I've been in your Watch House, I've seen what's in there.

Anne   Fair point.

Da Souza   I thought I'd pop in, find out how you were recovering from the Great Tynemouth Masquerade Ball. Was that young Master Timothy Jones I saw whisk you away?

Anne   Yes. He's weird.

Da Souza   Very weird. And I tell people to eat the Messiah once a week.

Anne   I like him. I think.

Da Souza   I'm glad. It will do him good to have a friend.

Anne   What about me?

Da Souza   I think you're considerably tougher than Timmo.

Anne   So I don't need friends?

Da Souza   Everyone needs friends, Anne. I'm hoping you might be mine.

Anne I thought you didn't know anything about women?

Da Souza I don't. But I know a lot about being a stranger in a new place. Feeling the ghosts we've left behind.

Anne Ghosts?

Da Souza *notices her reaction but doesn't understand. He points to the letter.*

Da Souza You must miss her. Your mother . . .

Anne Maybe. I don't know.

Da Souza No?

Anne It's not like she misses me. Couldn't wait to have me out of her hair.

Da Souza She said that?

Anne I can join up the dots.

Da Souza I'm sure you can. But, forgive me for being patronising, perhaps you don't see all the dots.

Anne It's obvious.

Da Souza Is it?

Anne Mum and Dad still talk. But if I come in, they shut up, get away as fast as they can.

Da Souza There are some things parents find too painful to speak about with their children.

Anne I've seen old photos, when they were happy.

Da Souza Anne, it's not –

Anne Don't bother. You're a priest, you shouldn't lie on my behalf.

She rips up the letter.

Pause.

Da Souza   Why don't you show me round this Watch House you're so keen on?

Anne   I thought you'd already seen it?

Da Souza   Not through your eyes.

Anne   Why don't you ask Arthur?

Da Souza   Arthur already has plenty of friends, he doesn't need another. Which means he doesn't see what you and I might see.

Anne *is a bit unsettled by this, unsure what he suspects.*

Anne   I don't know if I'm allowed. Prudie doesn't want me in there.

Da Souza   I'll square Prudie. She'll never say no to a man of the cloth, even if it's Roman.

Anne   OK, I guess.

She leads him out to the Watch House.

Do you want to see anything? The breeches buoy, the searchlight?

Da Souza *is silent. He's listening intently to the Watch House.*

Anne   Arthur says they're planning to build a sea path to the Fish Quay, prevent the risk of a landslide – he's got blueprints?

Da Souza *doesn't reply. He closes his eyes, breathes in – trying to sense something.*

Anne   What are you doing?

Da Souza (*not opening his eyes*)   Listening.

Pause.

Anne, is there anything you want to tell me?

Anne   Tell you?

Da Souza   Yes. As we're in this place together.

Anne   I don't know . . .

She hesitates. **Da Souza** *waits.*

Geordie *enters, unseen by either of them.*

Da Souza   Nothing you say will surprise me. I've been trained to believe the extraordinary. Anything you have to tell me, I will listen.

Anne   Anything?

Da Souza   Anything.

Pause.

You know where to find me if you change your mind.

He goes to leave, then stops.

Anne. The Watch House.

He wrestles to find the right words.

There's more danger on this hill than a potential landslide. Be careful. Please, be very careful.

He leaves. **Anne** *exhales and sits down.*

Geordie   Don't fret, hinny. Telling our truth . . . It can take a lifetime. Longer.

Timmo (*shouting offstage*)   Anne! Are you there?

Timmo *enters.*

Timmo   Aha! Where else would Anne Melton be, I asked myself, but the Watch House? Hypothesis: correct!

Anne   I'm not sure I'm in the mood, Timmo.

Timmo   No? No. Sorry.

He sits dejectedly beside her.

I never get people right.

Anne   I don't think I do either. Only the dead ones.

Timmo   That's what I've been ruminating upon!

Anne   What?

Timmo   Dead people. How to communicate with them. You had your vision – but you couldn't control that, could you? We need a better, more scientific method.

Anne   Do you ever see your point, Timmo, and think, 'Maybe today, just today, I'll try getting there'?

Timmo   All right. I present to you: Morse code!

Anne   Morse code?

Timmo   You said everyone in the Brigade learned it. And there's one thing The Old Feller is happy to use.

Anne   The lights . . .

Timmo   Give that woman a macaron! And what's one of your esteemed pal Timmo's many, many, perhaps endless skills? Morse code!

He brandishes a pen and paper.

Turn that lighthouse on, and let's see what The Old Feller has to say.

Anne *leaps up and does just that.*

At first, nothing unusual happens. The lights maintain a steady rhythm. **Timmo** *is scribbling on his pad, noting each flash.*

Geordie *closes his eyes. The audience may or may not notice his concentration.*

Anne   Come on, Old Feller, come on.

Timmo   Don't worry. This is a useful control. I'm establishing the base data set.

Anne   I wish I had a base data set to explain you.

Timmo   That's not how –

Anne   Shush!

The lights have changed. They start to flash, on and off, long and short.

Timmo (*as he scribbles, concentrating*)   A. N.

Geordie   H. E.

Timmo   L. P.

Geordie   Anne. Help.

Anne   That's the same as the message in the dust. It's The Old Feller!

She looks around, as if The Old Feller will reveal himself.

The lights flash again.

Timmo   W. A.

Geordie   R. E.

Timmo   H. A. G.

Geordie   U. E.

The lights return to their usual rhythm.

Anne   Is that it?

Timmo   I think so.

Anne *turns the lights off.*

Anne   So what's the message?

Timmo   W. A. R. E. H. A. G. U. E.

Geordie   Ware Hague.

Anne   That's all?

Timmo   That's all. An Help. Ware Hague.

Geordie   Ware Hague!

Timmo   Ware? What does that mean?

Geordie (*with increasing urgency*)   Anne. Help. Ware Hague!
Ware Hague!

Anne   It means beware.

The atmosphere should change, darken, threaten, become more chilling.

Timmo   Anne?

He sees that she's slipping away from him, entering a trance.

Anne   It's not just The Old Feller here.

Timmo   Come on, Anne, let's go.

He tugs at her hand. She doesn't move. She's staring straight ahead.

Geordie (*whimpering*)   Anne! He's here.

Anne   I see him. Oh God, I see him.

Timmo   Anne!

Anne   Scarlet coat. Blood red. And the skull.

Geordie   Flesh rolling away, falling like tears from
white bone.

Anne   He laughs. And he comes closer.

She reaches out her hand, as if to take him into her embrace.

Timmo   No, no!

He snaps the main lights on. Everything changes. If not normal, then not terrifying either.

Anne *comes back to herself.*

Anne   Hague.

Geordie (*whispering*)   Now she knows. Now, at last, she
understands.

Anne   The skull, worms writhing in the empty eyes, coming
to me. Coming for me.

Timmo   We're going, Anne. Right now.

He pulls her away.

Geordie   But he's still here. Anne!

Anne   The Old Feller! We can't leave him, not with Hague.

Timmo   Better him than us. Come on, MOVE.

He drags her out.

Geordie *is alone. He backs away, whimpering, arms raised over his head to protect himself. Something bears down on him.*

Geordie   Please. I beg you!

End of Act One.

Act Two

Scene One: An Overdue Introduction

The next morning at the Watch House – **Anne**'s *seventh in Tynemouth.*

Geordie *welcomes us back. He is definitely* **Geordie** *now, not* **Arthur**.

Geordie Perhaps you confused me for young Arthur? Don't reproach yourself, if you did. I should have had the manners to introduce meself properly. Henry Cookson, late of this parish. So late even young Arthur's drawing his pension. He was only a nipper when I knew him, now he's so bloody senile he's forgotten me name. The Old Feller, I ask you. I'd tan his hide if I weren't . . . well . . . deed.

Beat.

Mind you, that bairn's been a proper tonic. Breath o' fresh air.

He catches the eye of an audience member.

Aye, I know I can't breathe, mister, no need to be all hoity toity about it. Back in me Brigade days, we'd have wiped a smirk like yours off with a dunk in the sea.

He chuckles fondly, then grows gloomier.

Though we did worse than that. I saw it. I saw *him*.

Beat.

He's here, right now. Watching us. You can't feel him, can you? But I can. And Anne can. She's so close to the truth.

Anne *enters, followed by* **Timmo**.

Timmo Pray vouchsafe to me again, young Anne Melton, why we're coming back here?

Anne   Because the Watch House is the key. The answer is here. Who Hague is.

Timmo   I question your choices.

Anne   It's not a choice. I *must* do this.

Timmo   Modal verbs. My deadliest foe. Very well, Anne Melton, you compel me. Perhaps, if I'm lucky, The Old Feller will include me in his next dream of rotting corpses.

Anne   Timmo, don't mess around. Not in here.

Timmo   I jest not. I saw *Dawn of the Dead* six times. Mind you, I only paid twice. The Odeon usher's even slower than a zombie.

Anne   Don't you ever shut up?

Timmo   I –

Anne   Oh my God, it was rhetorical.

Timmo *mimes a silent – probably rude – reply.*

Anne   We need to find anything about Hague that we can. A record, photograph, anything.

Timmo   And then?

Anne   Then we can help The Old Feller to get rid of him.

They begin to peer around.

Timmo   I've been thinking –

Anne   You're meant to be looking.

Timmo   So fine a cognitive instrument as mine can do both. I juggle concepts like our friend Hague juggles skulls. And I keep wondering: why is The Old Feller reaching out to you?

Anne   Because I'm cute?

Timmo   And he's a dead pensioner, so that better not be the reason.

Anne   Jealous. Again. And you didn't deny I'm cute.

Timmo *is wrong-footed, for once.*

Timmo   Look, Anne, there has to be a reason why he's making contact with you. Why not Arthur? Why not any of the hundreds of people who've passed through here before you?

Anne   I don't know you well, Timmo, but I know that you never ask a question unless you think you've got an answer.

He hesitates.

This can't be any worse than telling me I'm a shit daughter.

Timmo   I didn't mean –

Anne   Just say it. Why you think The Old Feller is talking to me. Go on.

Timmo   All right . . . Your mum and dad have left. You can't talk to anyone you love, just strangers. You're alone. Like The Old Feller.

Anne *is upset.* **Geordie** *reaches out a hand towards her, then slowly lets it drop.*

Anne   So. I'm the saddest person ever in the Watch House, so pathetic even a ghost feels sorry for me and tries to be my mate.

Timmo   That isn't . . .

Anne   And you're all the same? Arthur, Prudie, Da Souza, you, you're all just pretending to be my friend. Scared I'll jump off the cliff?

Timmo   I've got this wrong . . .

Anne   Every time I see you, you insult me.

Timmo   I'm just shit with people. Hell, an actual ghost is better at making you understand him than I am.

Anne   And that's my fault?

Timmo   None of this is your fault!

Beat.

It's not because you're lonely. OK, maybe it is, but not just that. Because it means you understand people who are alone. That's why The Old Feller's reaching out to you. It's not because there's anything wrong with you. It's because you're so . . . right . . .

He runs out of steam, a tad lamely. **Anne** *is stunned.*

Geordie *alone seems happy. After a pause, he applauds. They can't hear him.*

Anne   That's really sweet. Is this your way of saying you . . . like me?

Timmo *retreats into science.*

Timmo   It's a tenable hypothesis.

Anne   Let me acquire more evidence then.

She slips her hand into his. Will they kiss?

Geordie   Ahem.

Geordie, *embarrassed, backs away and knocks something over – a brass plate, the one he begged* **Anne** *not to touch earlier, which falls with a clang.* **Anne** *breaks away to look.*

Anne   It's a plaque. About Hague! Oh, thank you Old Feller, thank you!

Timmo (*resentful*)   Yeah, thanks a metric tonne, Old Feller. Perfect timing.

Anne (*reading*)   'In memory of Major Scobie Hague, late of Her Majesty's 55th Regiment of Foot, who drowned while attempting the mercy of rescue, 14 October 1854. This monument was erected by his childhood sweetheart and his grieving friends.'

Timmo   His childhood sweetheart?

They half-grin, awkwardly, at each other.

Hague sounds like a hero.

Anne   Yet he's haunting The Old Feller. It doesn't make sense.

Timmo   Why isn't this on a gravestone at the Priory?

Anne   Because he isn't buried there. They mustn't have found his body.

Timmo   But we know where it is. Some of it.

Anne   The skull. It wants . . . *He* wants to be at rest.

Timmo   So we give it a proper burial.

Anne   Then he can leave the Watch House and The Old Feller will be free!

Geordie   No!

Timmo   We'll do it tonight, once it's dark enough to creep into the Priory. I don't fancy Da Souza or his sidekick Father Fletcher would welcome us muscling in on their business.

He sticks the skull up his jumper to hide it. **Geordie** *whimpers.*

Timmo   I'll bring a spade. Just a few hours and we'll be done.

Anne   Oh, Timmo, I feel so happy!

Timmo   Me too.

He grabs at **Anne**'s *hand. She's not expecting it and jumps.*

Timmo   Sorry!

Anne   You're all right. Just . . . A bit of warning?

Timmo (*despondently*)   OK.

Anne   I'll teach you to flirt if you teach me Morse code, deal?

Timmo   Deal!

He spits on his hand and extends it. She looks horrified. He retracts it hastily.

A verbal contract shall suffice.

Anne   It'll bloody have to!

Beat.

But why didn't The Old Feller pick that plaque out for us before?

Timmo   It's heavy. He might not have had the impetus to shift it until now.

Anne   What?

Timmo   One theory of the transfer of kinetic energy posits that –

Anne   Timmo.

Timmo   Basically, there's an idea that ghosts borrow the energy to move things from us. The Old Feller didn't have enough energy to shift this plaque, which must be a lot harder than just a few lights or some dust, until now.

Anne   Why now?

Timmo   Because it's only when we get really emotional they can feed from us. And, well, before . . .

Anne   I really like you, Timmo.

Timmo   Great!

Anne   But you do kind of ambush me with things?

Timmo   Oh. OK.

Beat.

I've got a spade to borrow. Apparently I've not finished digging holes for myself.

He exits.

Anne   Men!

Geordie   Anne. Not his bones. I beg you.

She doesn't hear. She trails after **Timmo***, exasperated.*

Geordie   Please. It's not of my doing. Please.

Geordie *backs away as something rises from Hague's spot.*

Scene Two: The Graves

Later the same day. **Anne**, **Arthur** *and* **Prudie** *are in the cottage, each occupied with their own affairs:* **Arthur** *puffing on his pipe,* **Prudie** *knitting,* **Anne** *reading a letter.*

Prudie   You must've read that letter from your ma a dozen times. You'll wear your eyes out.

Anne   I'm trying to figure out what I should write.

Prudie   Why, anything. I'm sure she'd be thrilled to hear from you, pet. I'll get some of the fancy paper in from that London feller next time I'm at the post office.

Anne   Oh no, I've a pad –

Prudie   I'll not hear of it! Miss Fiona receiving a letter on the paper Arthur uses to scribble his bets on, all reeking of fish.

Arthur   Give over, man. Bets and fish make life good. Here, lass, have you ever laid a bet?

Anne   No.

Arthur *digs in his pocket and hands her a coin.*

Arthur   Here you gan. Take that to the bookies, put it on any geegee takes your fancy.

Anne   Thanks!

Prudie   Arthur Herbert McGill! You're setting that bairn on the path to ruin!

Arthur   Am I thump. If it wins, she'll get a tidy payout. Why, a horse at 2–1 odds would return . . . it'd return . . .

Anne   A whole 20p.

Arthur   That'll keep us in treats for a week!

Anne   The words 'cost-of-living crisis' don't mean anything to you, do they Arthur?

Arthur   Eh?

Prudie   She's talking about *inflation*, you daft old sod. It's in every headline.

Arthur   There's nee inflation in fish. Now be away with you. Get that bet in.

Prudie   And pick up some paper, Miss Anne, save me old legs trogging up that hill.

Anne   OK.

Prudie   Besides, it will be good for you to be away from the Watch House and that Timmo Jones. He's an odd boy, Miss Anne.

Anne   For your information, it was Timmo's idea that I should write to my mum.

Arthur   I bet he's shared a few other ideas with you an' all.

Prudie   Arthur!

Anne (*colouring*)   All right! I'm going.

Arthur *and* **Prudie** *exit.*

Anne *walks up the hill. She passes the pony and stops.*

Anne   Any friendlier today?

She reaches out to pet it. The pony goes for her. Expecting it, **Anne** *steps back smartly.*

You're not the only savage animal around here, are you? Do you know that dog up in the Priory? I'd pay to watch you two go head to head.

Beat.

Actually . . . maybe that dog can show me a good spot. Somewhere quiet to lay Major Scobie Hague to rest. Rip out my jugular if you agree.

She reaches out, the pony lunges, she jumps back.

That's a yes then.

She moves on. The pony exits.

Geordie *enters, watching her wander through the graves. Now she's talking to the dog.*

Anne   Here, pup.

Geordie   Don't do it, Anne. Don't muck about with Hague's bones.

She finds a dug-up grave. Following their trail:

Anne   Pawprints! So you were here. Digging up poor old Joseph Beavers, foyboatman. His relatives would want you put down if they knew.

And Robert Johnson, river-pilot. What a mess you made of him.

Yet you haven't bothered with any other graves, not until . . . George Dobie, keelboatman.

Then it's . . . William Renshaw. Another foyboatman. And here: Samuel Hawke. Master's mate. OK, you've shown me where the ground's nice and soft to bury Hague.

Beat.

Christ, I'm talking to a pony and a dog. Maybe Timmo's right. Maybe I *am* that sad.

She retreats. Then she stops, as a thought hits her.

Those five . . .

Geordie   Beavers, foyboatman. Johnson, river-pilot. Dobie, keelboatman. Renshaw, foyboatman. Hawke, master's mate.

She retraces her steps and peers at the graves.

Anne   Died 1854. Died 1854. Died 1854. Died 1854. Died 1854. Oh no.

The dog howls offstage.

Geordie   Get out, lass. Back to Front Street, with its warm fuggy bookies and its fancy writing paper and its people, all its nice, normal people who don't care about a dog digging up five graves.

Timmo *enters, carrying a plastic bag and a spade.*

Anne   Timmo!

Timmo   Salutations – hey, what's wrong?

Anne   That dog.

Timmo   Canis Badis Boyis? It's known to prey on –

Anne   Graves. It's digging up sailors who died the same time as Hague.

Timmo   A regular Scooby-Doo.

Anne   Don't take the piss. It means something.

Timmo   It means good doggies deserve bones. Come on, let's put Scooby and Scobie together right now.

He pulls the skull from the bag and hefts the spade.

Geordie   Fool. You think that will hold him?

The dog howls.

Anne   I don't know about this.

Timmo   In the absence of a canine psychiatrist, we don't have any other option. Let's inter our budget Yorick.

They bury the skull. **Geordie** *watches, distressed.*

Anne   Should we say something?

Timmo   See you at Judgement Day, Major.

He sees **Anne** *is unsure.*

Timmo   Relax. It's over.

Beat.

Come on, I have plans for tonight.

He takes her hand, very elaborately so she isn't surprised, and they head off.

The dog howls, longer and more eerily. **Geordie** *crosses himself.*

Scene Three: A Bad Penny

The next morning, the eighth. **Anne***'s dancing to the radio in the cottage.*

Arthur *enters. She collides with him.*

Arthur   How, man. Don't mind me, I just live here.

Anne   Sorry, Arthur.

She turns the radio off.

I had the best night's sleep!

Arthur   You're in a grand mood. Is it that Timmo?

Anne   No! Well, not just him . . . I can't explain it, Arthur, but I just feel happy. Like I've sorted something out.

Arthur   Oh no, Miss Anne. You've gone and killed Prudie haven't you?

Anne   Hah. She's off to the shops – for more food, obviously.

Beat.

I really am grateful to you both. You . . . You've made me feel at home.

Arthur   Ah, haddaway and shite.

Anne   I mean it Arthur. Thank you.

Arthur   Aye, well . . . This is your home whenever you want it. And your ma's, if she ever comes to her senses and leaves that London.

Anne   Have you ever been to London, Arthur?

Arthur   Have I thump. I gut fish, not people. All them gangs and Tories.

Anne   Yes, shady groups of pinstriped men with quiffs, lurking in mood-lit Mayfair alleys.

Da Souza *enters, overhearing the last line.*

Da Souza   My, sounds like heaven. I'll have to borrow that image for my next sermon.

Arthur   Each to his own, Reverend, but that divvent sound like any Sunday school I know.

Da Souza   Dear Arthur, we can remedy even your stout soul with a mere swish of incense.

Arthur   Incense? I live with me sister, like, but strictly separate rooms. Nee truck with any funny business.

Anne   No, Arthur, that's not –

Arthur   Nee judgement here, pet, but I best be off.

He leaves.

Da Souza   I fear that's one I'll never convert. To any of my ways of thinking.

Anne   I'd like to see you try.

Da Souza   I actually came not to try my luck with Arthur but you.

Anne   Well, here I am.

Da Souza   Yes, here you are.

Anne   I'm still writing that letter to my mum, if you –

Da Souza   Anne.

Anne   You're worried, aren't you? But look at me. I'm fine.

Da Souza   I'm not so sure. I'm not your only unexpected visitor.

He pulls something from his robe. The skull.

This was on the step.

Anne *says nothing. She won't take it, so* **Da Souza** *lays it down gently.*

Da Souza   Please, talk to me.

Anne   I need to see Timmo.

Da Souza   That boy is not equipped to handle whatever's going on here. Nor are you. Listen, I could call the police, report human remains, have them crawling all over the Watch House. But that will only antagonise whatever it is that confronts you. Let me help.

She hesitates.

This is dangerous. I can't protect you if you won't share what's happening.

Anne   Protect me?

Da Souza   Whatever is going on here, it frightens me. This (*pointing at skull*) isn't some Halloween jape. It's the ruins of a human being.

Anne (*whispers*) We buried it.

Da Souza   And something brought it back.

Anne   The dog.

Da Souza   Animals are easily swayed. They're more receptive to . . . undue influence.

Anne   I told Timmo there was something wrong.

Da Souza   Laying someone to rest isn't as simple as digging a couple of feet then spreading earth on top. There are words to be said, prayers to be offered. Especially if the body is not whole. Something so fractured and restless cannot be confined by mere mud.

Anne   We needed to bury it all? Not just the skull?

Da Souza   Anne. It's not a puzzle you can solve by joining all the pieces. There's a spirit, something metaphysical, which must be healed. I've felt it. In the Watch House. I know you have too. But unless you confide the truth in me, I cannot help.

Anne   You wouldn't believe me. No one would. Only a weirdo like Timmo.

Da Souza   I'm pretty weird too, you know.

Anne   I don't even know how to start . . . (*She takes a breath, then in a rush.*) There are two ghosts, one called The Old Feller only his real name's Henry Cookson and he's good, he's really good, but there's another called Major Scobie Hague who haunts The Old Feller, really cruel, really horrible, and that's his skull, Major Hague's skull, which we wanted to bury to stop him. Only that dog's digging up the same five graves, all sailors who died the same time as Hague, so there must be something more to how he died. That's why he keeps coming back.

Beat.

Do you . . . Do you think I'm mad?

Da Souza   Not at all. That sounds entirely sane. Two restless, unhappy souls, one bullying the other. I see that every day in my parish. Though they're usually alive. And married.

Anne   The Old Feller deserves better. Hague's ruining his . . .

Da Souza   Afterlife? Listen, Anne. It's not just Hague. I'll swear to it that The Old Feller has his own regrets. Happy people tend not to linger after death. Or to be easily persecuted – that's why bullies, like this Hague, go after the vulnerable.

Anne   You think The Old Feller has a secret?

Da Souza   I'm certain of it. To bring peace to Henry Cookson, you must heal whatever pain's inside him. Only then can Hague be banished.

Anne   How?

Da Souza   You tell me. It's you The Old Feller's chosen.

Anne   Me?

Da Souza   I only pray, when he makes his truth known, that you'll come straight to me. I implore you. For your own safety, not just Henry Cookson's.

Scene Four: On the Rocks

Later that day. **Timmo** *and* **Anne** *are on the Black Middens.*

Timmo   So this turbulent priest says: 'Young Anne Melton, I don't have a clue what's going on, not a shadow of an iota of a wisp of a soupçon of a clue, but I promise I can help. Tell me all, then I'll claim the credit and get a juicy bone from the bishop.'

Anne   And then you went: 'Incredible Anne Melton, I can't tolerate anyone else having your attention, so ignore everything that priest said and come with me to the Middens this instant.'

Timmo   You missed out how witty and charming I was.

Anne   It's easily missed. What's your grand plan then?

Timmo   Another episode of 'Spooks'!

Anne   'Spooks' is a stupid name for a show. It'd never catch on.

Timmo   'Undead News', whatever. But this is where you had the first vision, right here. We'd rowed, which gave The Old Feller enough energy to break through to you.

Anne   So try that again, see if we find something else out to stop Hague?

Timmo   A few ideas did present themselves about how we work up the energy this time . . .

Anne   Well, they can unpresent themselves, mister.

Timmo   In that case, the postman just gave me this, save him trudging up the hill. It should do the trick.

He produces a formal-looking letter. She snatches it.

Anne   The trick? You know what this is?

Timmo   I recognised the seal.

Anne   And you've just sat on it with your fat arse?

Timmo   I figured we might as well make it useful.

Anne   There's no 'we' about this Timmo.

Timmo   We're . . . friends.

Anne   Friends respect each other.

Timmo *doesn't have an answer.* **Anne** *opens the letter and reads.*

Geordie *enters.*

Anne   They're officially divorced.

Timmo   I'm sorry, Anne.

Anne   I hope that's *useful* enough.

Timmo   Are you . . . OK?

Anne   OK? My parents have split. You think I should be OK?

Timmo   No –

Anne   You don't care anyway. You betrayed me.

She moves away. **Geordie** *follows her.*

Timmo   Anne?

She stands still, facing dead ahead. **Timmo** *stops, unnerved.*

Anne   I'm here. Above the rocks.

Geordie   I'm here. A little bairn, barely ten, snuck out after bedtime to see the storm.

Anne   The rain pours, so thick you can't see through the driving, whipping lines. A ship rears and bucks, helpless on the waves, ropes snapping like bones.

Geordie   At its prow a huge white figurehead, of a warrior with shield and spear. I divvent know what it's called, but the gleam in the dark makes me shiver.

Anne   It's a Greek warrior. This is *The Hoplite*.

Geordie   All the way from Australia, now sinking in her own river. The law-abiding folks know there's nowt to be done, for this is long before the Brigade exists. So they go to church. And they pray.

Anne   Only wreckers remain. They'll rob whatever washes ashore – luggage, cargo, bodies.

Geordie   I'm quaking down to me bloody boots. I hide in a crack in the rocks.

Anne   *The Hoplite*'s lifeboats are smashed to pieces as soon as they're lowered into that pulsing sea. There's no escape.

Geordie   Then one man dives into the waves, a rope tied around his waist. Huge feller, all muscle. Even in the moonlight I can see the red coat. A soldier.

Anne   If he can swim to shore, that rope might just be fixed so the others can follow. It's a brave, impossible mission.

Geordie   But he makes it. Somehow he stumbles on to these rocks, inches from my hiding spot. Beneath his arm, a small iron box. He clings to it like it's the Holy Grail. He's made it. He's hyem.

Anne   Then the wreckers appear.

Geordie   Beavers – foyboatman. Johnson – river-pilot. Dobie – keelboatman. Renshaw – foyboatman. Hawke – master's mate.

Anne   The soldier puts up a brave fight. He takes two of the wreckers with him, caving their heads in with that iron box, but the rest close in.

Geordie   They do for him, so near I can feel his dying breath.

Anne   They cut the rope loose. With it any chance to save the ship. Then they turn to the box.

Geordie   He's strapped it to his wrist with iron chains, to make sure the sea divvent get it.

Anne   So they cut his hand off.

Geordie   Long white fingers twitching then falling still, like worms wriggling into the mud.

Anne   It's a pay chest. The soldier's stolen it. They snatch all the gold. Then they stuff the hand in and push the box into the rocks.

Geordie   To me. It comes to me.

Anne   They bury his body. He gets no more than a shallow grave, for the tide is turning. Their own dead they carry away.

Geordie   Major Scobie Hague, a brave man and a wretched thief, murdered before my eyes. And I . . . I went to close that box, to snap the lid shut on its horror. But I saw one last gold sovereign, caught between those cold wet fingers. I took it, God forgive me, I tugged it free and I kept it. Then I left that box there and ran home. I never told a soul. Never.

Anne   Until now.

Geordie *slumps, head in hands.*

Anne *comes to. She and* **Timmo** *are both shocked by what she saw.*

Timmo   Anne?

Anne   I saw it all.

Timmo   I didn't expect . . .

Pause. She gathers herself with an effort.

Anne   Those graves. Two Hague killed. The others soon after . . . He must have got them too.

Timmo   It's awful. But just think what we've learned.

Anne   I'm too tired for this.

Timmo   Hague's bones are here!

Anne   Fine, we know where his bones are.

Timmo   They're just a few inches down. A shallow grave.

He digs at the mud, using his bare hands. **Anne** *watches, tired.*

Anne   It's not just about getting his body together. Da Souza said that wouldn't be enough.

Timmo   How would he know? We're going to find Major Scobie Hague, then we're going to put him to rest once and for all.

Anne   Don't you have a spade?

Timmo   Had to give it back to my father, for his precious allotment.

Anne   That mud's filthy, all pebbles and shells. You'll destroy your hands.

Timmo   I'm not waiting any longer, not with what this is doing to you.

Anne   Is that really the reason, Timmo?

Timmo   Of course it is.

Anne   It's not that you're desperate to be the one to figure out the solution, to prove Da Souza wrong and you right?

Timmo *keeps digging but he won't look at her now.*

Anne   Because you brought me here and put that letter into my hand. You wrung the sadness out of me for The Old Feller to feed on.

Timmo   You don't believe that.

Anne   I think your hurry to dig Hague up is because you're always in a race against yourself. How clever can Timmo Jones be this time? How quickly can he find the answer, get full marks? My feelings are just data to you.

Timmo   I'd never do anything to hurt you –

Anne   That's what my mum and dad said. Then this. (*She waves the letter.*) Divorce. Custody. No one gives a shit about me.

Timmo   Custody? Anne – will you stay here?

Anne   Are you asking because you care, or because you want to monitor me like some lab specimen, work out when you can next wring the misery out of me for another vision?

Timmo   You asked me to help you save The Old Feller. That's what I'm doing.

Anne   You've just hit me with the worst news of my life, and I'm meant to be grateful?

Timmo   No. But logically, we're now –

Anne   Why are you trying to make this logical? This is my life!

Beat.

I let you in. I let you in, and you're using me. You're just some freak who's latched onto me because no one else wants him.

Timmo *finally stops digging.*

Timmo   I don't want to lose another friend.

Anne   It's too late, Timmo. You've drained the life out of me.

Timmo   I thought it would help, draw out The Old Feller. I didn't think about you being hurt.

Anne   Join the club.

Timmo   What does that mean?

Anne   It means anyone unlucky enough to know me becomes the worst version of themselves. Mum and Dad, you, even these bloody ghosts. It's me.

Beat.

I want to go home. Home home. Because this doesn't feel like it. Not even close to it.

Timmo   Anne, I . . .

He sees a glint where he's been digging.

I've got something.

Geordie *finally looks up.*

Anne   Good for you, Timmo.

She stands up and walks away. **Timmo** *pulls out bones. Human bones.*

Geordie *stands up, alarmed.*

Timmo   Hague must have been huge! Anne, wait!

Anne   Leave me alone.

Geordie   You need to be calm, lass.

Timmo   But Anne, we can finish this now! Don't you see?

Anne   Fuck off!

Geordie   Anne! Don't get riled, not here.

Anne   I'm through with this. With you, with The Old Feller, all of you.

She leaves. **Timmo** *follows, clutching the bones.*

Geordie   Not that way.

A noise, a shifting and rumbling of the earth. **Anne** *and* **Timmo** *stop and look up, fearful.*

Timmo   The hillside. It's . . . it's moving.

Geordie   Run!

Timmo *drops the bones. They scarper. The noise is overpowering – everything has collapsed. Until, slowly, a ringing turns to silence.*

Scene Five: Recovery

An hour later. **Anne** *and* **Timmo** *are in foil emergency blankets, holding polystyrene cups of tea. Clearly the rescue services are on the scene.*

Geordie *has vanished.*

Timmo   That was awesome.

Anne *doesn't respond.*

Timmo   Witnessing a landslide? Awesome.

Still no response.

It's a landslide, not an earthquake, because Tynemouth doesn't sit on any tectonic boundary plates. Hence the ground must have given way because of –

Anne   A ghost. That's what caused this, Timmo, and you know it. Not subsidence or excessive rainfall or whatever else the evening news will say, but a ghost.

Pause.

It's my fault. I lost my temper and Hague used that energy to try to murder us.

Timmo   You still don't come close to winning the trophy for biggest dickhead of the day. I'm sorry, Anne. I messed up, with the letter, with the bones, with you.

Anne   For a self-declared genius, you're pretty stupid.

Timmo   I've come to that conclusion.

Beat.

I dropped the bones. They're under all those tonnes of rubble. Hague is buried more deeply now than he ever was on the Middens.

Anne   You don't fancy another go?

Timmo   Even my dad's best shovel wouldn't do the trick. Hague's beyond our reach. It's over.

Anne   The poor Old Feller.

Timmo   I'm sorry.

Anne   Timmo Jones. Thank you for trying.

Timmo   Anne Melton. Thank you for letting me.

She smiles at him, gently.

Anne   We rushed headlong into things and made a terrible mess, didn't we?

Timmo   Are you talking about the ghosts, or us?

Anne   Both.

Beat.

I'm sorry I called you a freak, Timmo.

Timmo   Would holding hands be too much right now?

Anne   You're getting the hang of it. I think we just need to be mates for a while, OK?

Timmo   OK.

Arthur *enters. He's distraught.*

Arthur   Thank Christ. I thought you bairns were goners.

Anne   It's all right, Arthur. Not even a bruise.

Arthur *pats them each, as close to showing affection as he can manage.*

Arthur   At least Prudie can't blame me for a ruddy landslide.

Anne   No, this one is all on me.

Arthur   Eh? You didn't take a knock to the heed, did you, pet?

Timmo   Fear not, Arthur. It takes more than a mere splitting of the Earth to undo Anne Melton.

Arthur   Well, you're right as rain, spouting off as always. Seems me poor pony's the only casualty.

Anne   Oh no, Arthur.

Arthur   He fell from the cliff. Lucky the whole damn Watch House didn't follow.

Anne   What a loss. He was . . . He was . . .

Arthur   He was a bugger, Miss Anne, a reet bugger. But I'll miss him. Can't even say goodbye, with him buried under all that. They'd dig a person out in double quick time, but they divvent give a toss about a pony.

Timmo   Say that again, Arthur.

Arthur   What? They rescue people, not animals. Not even a Gallower.

Timmo   Yes! They'll have to dig if anyone's buried under that.

Arthur (*sharply*)   You mean there's someone under there?

Timmo   Not anyone living, Arthur, calm down. But bones. A veritable ossuary of bones. And the police are legally bound to dig them up – then rebury them!

He runs off.

Arthur   Bones?

Anne   We'll explain later, Arthur. But you've given us the best news.

Arthur   You nippers is nearly killed, find out me pony's a goner, then go daffy over digging up some bones. Maybe Prudie's right. Maybe you are all on drugs.

Anne   You wouldn't believe some of the trips I've had, Arthur. But don't worry. It's not what you think.

Beat.

I'm sorry again about your pony.

*She gives **Arthur** a peck on the cheek, then exits after **Timmo**.*

Arthur *turns to the mound of rubble.*

Arthur   Bye, you old bugger. Next time I see a bairn with a finger missing, I'll think of you.

Scene Six: The Sermon

The next day – **Anne***'s ninth in Tynemouth.* **Da Souza** *is alone in the cottage. He's reading a newspaper, clearly for the umpteenth time, and seems agitated.*

Anne *enters, in her pyjamas.*

Da Souza   At last!

Anne   It's not even 9 a.m. If this is Vespers, I don't like it.

Da Souza   Vespers is the evening prayer, you horrid little agnostic. I'm here because of this.

He flings the newspaper down. **Anne** *peers at it.*

Anne   Tory councillor caught in bed with haddock?

Da Souza   Other side.

He flips it round.

A double spread on the landslide and a set of old bones the police retrieved, following a tip-off by one Timothy Jones, a sixth former at King's School. What have you done?

Anne   You might ask how we are.

Da Souza   I know how you are. Pig-headed, ignorant, insufferable meddlers!

Anne   Father, it's all right. Now the coroner has Hague's bones, they'll bury him and give him the peace he needs.

Da Souza   For the love of all ten of Ignatius's toe nails. I explicitly told you that bringing Hague's bones together won't exorcise him. It just makes him stronger, more malevolent.

Anne   At least we did something.

Da Souza   Oh, you did something. A litany of disasters befell those bones en route to the coroner. First, a police car carrying them crashed. Then they used a cyclist, who was attacked by a dog – yes, our canine friend. When they finally reached the morgue, a fire broke out!

Anne   But surely once they're properly laid to rest –

Da Souza   You little fool. The body is no more than a repository, for our hopes, our sins, our pain. Yes, they'll bury his remains after they've poked and prodded them, but what good will that do? You don't heal a broken heart by sticking a band-aid on the chest. And that's what Hague is. A broken, wounded spirit, one that lives outside those bones – he doesn't seek rest, but revenge.

Anne   I need to find Timmo.

Da Souza   That boy's done enough damage. He won't do any more.

Anne   What do you mean?

Da Souza   I persuaded his father to send Timmo to stay with relatives.

Anne   You did what!

Da Souza   That boy's fingerprints are all over this mess. I'll protect you despite yourselves.

Anne   Timmo protects me –

Da Souza   Does he, Anne? Do you truly believe that?

Anne   How dare you claim to know what I believe.

Da Souza   Timmo can't help you, not with this. You're beyond the limits of science now.

Arthur *enters.*

Arthur   Pyjamas on one, robes on the other. Fancy dress party is it?

No response.

Something the matter?

Anne   Get him to leave me alone.

Da Souza   Oh, pull yourself together –

Arthur   That's enough o' that.

Da Souza   Damn it, Arthur, you've no idea what's at stake.

Arthur   I divvent pretend to be a clever man, Reverend, but I know one thing. This is her home, not yours. You've an entire church to prattle on in. You'd best get back to it.

Da Souza   Christ preserve me. Anne, there are some things not even Arthur can protect you from. You'll realise that soon enough.

Da Souza *exits*.

Arthur   A'reet, hinny?

No answer.

I divvent mind, but if I'm going to hell on yer behalf, it only seems fair that you look at me.

Anne   I'm sorry, Arthur.

Arthur   Nowt to apologise for. I'm not harbouring any wish to be an altar boy, not at my time o' life. I'll gan after the Baptists next, if you like.

He shadow boxes. She smiles.

Anne   Thanks, Arthur.

Arthur   What was all that about? I thought Da Souza was a bit of a favourite of yours?

Anne   He's had Timmo sent away!

Arthur   Ah.

Beat.

You still got that Brigade badge, pet?

Anne   Yes.

She digs it out.

Arthur   Blimey, even carry it in yer pyjamas. Can't say I ever went that far meself. Well, lass, look: that shows that you're one o' us. Just as Timmo is. A born-and-bred Tynemouth lad, for all he's away wi' the fairies half the time.

Anne So?

Arthur So, even if you're apart, you're still bonded by that. And not just with Timmo, neither, but every man jack of the Brigade as ever lived. You've got all o' us with you. No one, not even a priest, can undo that.

Anne Thank you, Arthur. That's something I really needed to hear.

Beat.

I've got to go.

She exits. **Arthur** *shouts after her:*

Arthur At least change out o' yer ruddy pyjamas first!

Scene Seven: Communion

A few minutes later. **Geordie** *is in the Watch House.*

The lights flicker wildly. Though we can't see him, we should understand that Hague is present too, by the way **Geordie** *cowers. He's muttering to himself.*

Geordie Anne. Help. Ware Hague. Anne. Help.

The lights flicker even more madly, then cut out. Darkness.

Anne *enters, back in normal clothes.*

Anne Old Feller? Henry? Are you there? You are, aren't you. Listen, Old Feller, listen carefully. Can you . . . Can you tell me, what it is you need? If burying Hague –

Geordie *whimpers at the name, the lights flicker and perhaps hiss.*

Anne Sorry – if burying him doesn't bring an end, then it must be what Da Souza said. It must be something in you that needs healing. Is that it, Henry? Some burden I need to ease?

Geordie *stretches out his hand but cannot connect.*

Anne   I need you to show me what it is.

The lights flicker.

Timmo's the one who knows Morse code, not me.

The lights flicker one last time then go out.

I don't know how to help. Unless . . . I'll say something, and if I'm right, you flick the light. If I'm wrong, don't. You got that, Old Feller?

Geordie *looks up, hopefully. The lights flicker.*

Anne   OK, OK . . . Is it you I need to heal, not Hague?

The lights flicker.

Is it something you need to tell someone, a message to pass on?

Nothing.

Is it something to do with your descendants?

No lights.

What about something hidden, I need to find?

The lights flicker.

What is it? No, you can't answer that . . . How about: is it close?

The lights flicker again.

Here? In the Watch House?

Nothing.

The Middens?

The lights flicker.

We're almost there, Old Feller, we're so close.

Geordie *suddenly looks away, fearful. Hague is closing in.*

Anne   If I find it, should I bring it here?

No response; **Geordie** *is shrinking away from Hague.*

Anne   Henry?

Geordie   Anne. Ware Hague.

Anne   That's a no . . .

Geordie   Ware Hague!

Anne   Do I take it to someone?

Geordie *drops to his knees. The lights flicker intensely – Hague is attacking them, though* **Anne** *doesn't yet realise.*

Anne   Woah, OK, that's got you excited.

She grows concerned as the lights fire ever more furiously.

All right, I get it . . . Old Feller?

Geordie   Run. Leave.

The lights are now blazing. **Anne** *has to shield her eyes.*

Anne   It's him, isn't it?

Geordie *curls up in pain.*

Anne   All right, Hague. I'm not scared of you!

The lights suddenly cut out, and there's an almighty crash. Hague has shattered the model. **Geordie** *screams in pain.*

Da Souza *runs on.*

Da Souza   Anne! Anne, are you in here?

He finds her and shields her. Then he turns to address the Watch House.

Enough! Enough of you, Major Scobie Hague. You've done enough damage today!

Hague goes. **Geordie** *slowly uncurls. The darkness lessens a smidge.*

Da Souza *turns back to* **Anne.**

Da Souza   Are you all right?

Anne (*shakily*)   Are you following me?

Da Souza   I admit I am. But just as well. Or you might have ended up in as many pieces as that lighthouse.

Anne   Oh, poor Arthur.

Da Souza   He can glue it back together. We've bigger things to worry about.

Anne   I'm still not talking to you.

Da Souza   Fair enough. But may I talk to you?

Anne *says nothing.*

Da Souza   I'll take that as a yes. I'm sorry, Anne. You're dealing with something unimaginable, and I didn't have the courage to face it with you. Whatever's in this Watch House, I knew I wasn't strong enough, because it leaches its power from guilt like mine. So I scolded and fussed and tried to discourage you, and only pushed us further apart.

Beat.

But I hope you understand? I think you, better than anyone I've ever met, know what it is to find the people you care about being pushed away, despite your best intentions. I'm hoping that means you can forgive me. Can you, Anne?

Silence. **Geordie** *moves closer.*

Finally, she pulls out a letter. Turning it over in her hands, staring at it, she speaks.

Anne   I felt so relieved when I saw those bones dug out, like a great weight was gone. I thought that was it. I thought I'd saved The Old Feller. I just came home, sat down and wrote to my mother, like it was the easiest thing in the world. After all this time, the agony just went and I could tell her how I feel.

Da Souza   I'm so glad.

Anne   But I don't think I'll ever be the person who wrote that letter, not after this. I can't send it. Mum would read it so happily, but it would be from a different daughter, one she'll never meet. I had a glimpse of who I'd like to be, and just for a moment I could express it, get it all down on paper. Now it's gone. I've ruined The Old Feller's last chance. I've failed him.

Geordie   Dear Anne.

Unconsciously prompted by **Geordie**, *she comes to a decision.*

Anne   I forgive you.

Geordie *smiles.*

Da Souza   Thank you, Anne.

Beat.

You won't welcome this insight, and I'm only a silly priest, but you're still very young. It's the young who feel things most keenly. You feel guilty for things that aren't your fault, because you've not yet learned there are some things we can't control. But Hague isn't persecuting The Old Feller because of you. And your parents aren't divorcing because of you.

Anne   You don't know –

Da Souza   I do, Anne. Trust me, their reluctance to share what they're going through isn't because they blame you. It's because they love you. They're trying to protect you.

Beat.

Some kinds of love can only speak through silence. A man like me knows that. Just as I know how guilt can eat a person up.

Pause.

Anne   I think I've never seen you as anything except an adult, Father, and that's not fair is it?

Da Souza Life isn't fair, Anne. But it's better for having people like you in it.

Beat.

You're not to blame for any of this, you know. For your parents and Hague and The Old Feller. You need to relinquish your guilt.

Anne (*slowly*) A young person who grew up with guilt. Who never let it go.

Da Souza My pep talk doesn't extend to indulging spoken word.

Anne The Old Feller. As a kid, he witnessed Hague's murder, then he stole the last coin from the corpse. That's what made him who he is – all that guilt, it's what drove him to found the Brigade, to rescue all those people, to stay behind in the Watch House after death. He's trapped by guilt. And he hid it away, buried it, so no one could find it.

Da Souza I'm afraid I regard cod psychology about as positively as teenage poetry.

Anne Don't you see? You were right, Father: there is something which keeps The Old Feller here. That's why Hague haunts him. That's it, isn't it, Henry?

Geordie *nods*.

Da Souza Anne. You think we can heal The Old Feller?

Anne And send Hague packing at the same time, yes. You don't mind getting your feet wet, do you?

Scene Eight: Lives and Deaths

Back on the Middens. **Geordie** *is alone with the waves and the gulls*.

Geordie It'll take them a while to get to the Middens, but not me. One of the perks of me situation, travelling faster than a schooner in a gale. One of the few perks. So I've had some time to think.

Beat.

Hague may have been a thief, but he stole only from the army; I stole from a murdered man. I deserve his vengeance. I should never have asked Anne to help. It was weak.

Anne, *followed by* **Da Souza**, *comes stumbling over the rocks. They can't see/hear* **Geordie**.

Da Souza   Lord, you're testing me, your humble servant, and I gladly endure for my faith in thee is pure. But must you also test these loafers? They're Gucci.

He lifts his bedraggled feet, sadly. **Anne** *arrives at a crack in the rocks.*

Anne   Here. This is where they killed Hague and stowed the iron box. That's what The Old Feller wants me to find.

Da Souza   Surely it's not still there?

Anne   Why else would The Old Feller send me visions here?

Da Souza   Well, you do the honours. Too many years living off fat tithes mean I can't squeeze in there.

Anne *wriggles in.* **Geordie** *follows her.*

Geordie   I should never have brought this on you.

Da Souza   Is there anything?

Anne   I've got it! I've got it!

Geordie *carries the box out.* **Anne** *talks as if she's carrying it, but we see him do so. She examines it as he holds it.*

Anne   God, it's rusted right through. The lid's crumbled to nothing.

Da Souza   Anne. Before you lift that, what are you expecting?

Anne   I don't know. But let's find out.

Anne *opens the box.* **Geordie** *moans in distress.*

Anne   It's . . . bones. Hague's hand. So tiny, like little birds. And there's gold. Lots of gold!

She pulls out a fistful of coins.

And . . . a note, in an oilcloth.

She opens it. **Geordie** *recites aloud, pained by each word.*

Geordie   I have paid in full. God have mercy. Henry Cookson. 1903.

Anne   There's a fortune, far more than the coin he took.

Da Souza   Atonement. Through a life of service with the Brigade, then by repaying the debt.

Anne   But it wasn't enough, was it?

Geordie   Not nearly enough.

Anne   How cruel. What more did he have to do?

Da Souza   Forgive himself. And he can't.

Anne   But I can.

She pulls out a letter.

Da Souza   What are you doing?

Anne   Giving Hague the chance to finish this.

She reads.

'A friend told me I should start this with "Hi", because I couldn't find the right word for what you are to me. But then I realised there's no single word for that. You're my mother, and you're my protector. You're my mum, and you're my friend. You were Fiona McGuire, then you became Fiona Melton, and soon you will be Fiona McGuire again, but whatever your name, you'll always be the most important person in my life. Yet we've hurt each other, again and again. I can only say I'm sorry. You don't need to say you're sorry, because I know that already. All I hope you'll say is that I can come home soon, wherever that is, because home is where you are. All my love, your daughter, Anne.'

Pause. **Da Souza** *and* **Geordie** *should be moved.* **Anne** *recovers herself.*

Anne   Come on, Major. That's everything. All I have to feel. Use it. Show yourself.

Geordie   Dear girl.

Geordie *reaches out and – at last – manages to touch her. Her head snaps up and she sees him. There is a moment, in which time slows, and they look at one another. Everything* **Geordie** *now says,* **Anne** *will hear.* **Da Souza** *will not.*

Anne   Henry.

Geordie (*quietly*)   Save yourself, Anne.

Hague is upon us.

Anne   He's here.

She steps forward, to face Hague.

Da Souza   I feel him. I feel him, but I cannot see him.

Anne   Only I can.

Geordie   Leave her be!

He tries to come to her but can't, forced back by Hague.

Da Souza   Our father, who art in heaven, hallowed be thy name . . .

He continues reciting the Lord's Prayer under his breath, but struggles. He sinks to his knees.

Anne   I see you, Major Hague. And I know you see me.

She staggers back, as if hit.

Geordie   Anne!

He flails towards her, is rebuffed, then falls to his knees alongside **Da Souza**.

Anne   You can't hurt me. I have friends: Arthur, Prudie, Timmo, Da Souza. And I have The Old Feller, Henry Cookson. And he has me.

The oppression increases, darker, louder, nastier.

I know that my mother and my father's problems are not mine. They're in pain, and afraid, but that's not my fault. They love me! I forgive them!

It gets even more intense and furious.

And I forgive you, Major Scobie Hague. Whatever your crime, you were a brave man and deserved better.

She's shouting now, at the extreme limit.

The Old Feller is not the one who wronged you. You know he is innocent, as I am innocent. You cannot hurt me, and you cannot hurt him. Because he is not guilty. He is my friend.

Geordie *crawls to her. He holds up the box.*

Geordie   Anne.

Anne   I pay whatever debt he owes you with that friendship.

She lifts up the Brigade badge and drops it into the box. Above the noise and fury, it should ring with a resolute echo.

Then silence. Sudden, blissful silence.

Hague is gone.

Slowly, **Geordie** *stands.* **Da Souza** *is still kneeling, overcome; he won't hear what follows.*

Geordie (*wonderingly*)   He's gone?

Anne   He's gone. There was nothing left for him.

Geordie *embraces her. Gently, she disengages.*

Anne It's time you went too, Henry. With my love and my friendship and my thanks for everything you've taught me: go.

Geordie *smiles at her, touches her hand, then exits.*

Anne *is exhausted. She sits.*

Da Souza *crawls to sit beside her.*

Da Souza I have the feeling something extraordinary happened, just beyond my comprehension.

Anne Nothing extraordinary. Just what we all try to do every day. Forgive each other.

Da Souza *nods and takes a deep breath.*

Da Souza That was a hell of a letter you wrote your mother.

Scene Nine: Goodbye

[*The manner in which this last scene is played will depend on whether the production has involved doubling; some optional dialogue is included in brackets if it has.*]

It's **Anne***'s last day in Tynemouth. She's alone in the Watch House.*

Anne It's so quiet. The Watch House won't be the same without you. Both of you, Henry Cookson, Major Scobie Hague.

Arthur *and* **Prudie** *enter, bickering.*

Arthur You've got to take your arms off the bairn some time, woman!

Prudie Oh, Miss Anne!

She falls on **Anne***, sobbing and clutching her.*

Arthur The lass isn't dead, for crying out loud! She's only away to London.

Prudie   You callous brute. It's words like that that have driven her away.

Anne   No one's driven me away, Prudie. You've both been wonderful. But it's time for me and Mum to be together.

Prudie *stifles her sobs. A new thought hits.*

Prudie   Miss Fiona and Miss Anne, together. That's nice.

Anne   It is Prudie, it really is.

Prudie's *still calculating.*

Prudie   And it's a long journey to London. You'll be driving through elevenses, dinner, tea and maybe even supper, if traffic's bad. Four meals missed. Four!

Anne   No, not –

Arthur   Hush, let her get it out.

Prudie   You'll be starving, poor lambs! But I know how to sort you out, my loves. Don't worry, Prudie will look after you!

She gives **Anne** *a quick hug and rushes out.*

Anne   Will she be OK?

Arthur   Divvent worry. She'll sob her eyes out for a few more hours, then remember it's the church fete tomorrow and she's on cooking rota. That'll perk her up.

Anne   Did Father Da Souza ask her to do that?

Arthur   Aye. I'm coming round to him, like.

Anne   He's one of my favourite Tynemouth men. The others being you and Timmo.

Arthur   A priest, a lad and a pensioner. Prudie's reet. You need to get out more.

Anne   I think I spent my time perfectly.

Arthur   Welcome back whenever you fancy.

Anne   Oh, I will be. I've unfinished business with Timmo.

Arthur   I divvent know if I should allow it, but he's coming in an' all.

Anne   He's back?

Arthur   Aye, his aunt endured him for two days then broke down. He arrived and marched straight here, demanding to see you. Gave me some gabble about civil rights. Told him, I've heard of haddock and cod, never habeas corpus. (*Shouting.*) All right then, in yer come!

Timmo *enters.* **Arthur** *retreats to give them space.*

Timmo   Anne Melton!

They hover awkwardly.

I'll never forgive that old fraud Da Souza for denying me the grand finale.

Anne   He was right, Timmo. He gave me the answer I needed, in the end.

Timmo   I wish I could have.

Anne   It's good for you to lose once in a while.

Timmo   That's a hypothesis I must disprove.

Beat.

I'll miss you. I might even go and visit old Scobie's grave, now he's finally in there.

Anne   Aren't you worried about that dog?

Timmo   It's safely at Longbenton Animal Shelter.

Anne   I'm glad it's been rescued.

Timmo   Of course you are. You rescue whatever crosses your path, don't you?

Beat.

Bye, Anne Melton. Until we meet again.

They hug, at last. **Timmo** *exits.*

Arthur   I divvent pretend to follow half of what yis are on about, but he's a good lad at heart.

Da Souza *enters* [*still changing from* **Timmo**'s *exit, if doubling; if so, play it up, panting, etc.*].

Da Souza   Was that young Timmo Jones who hared past me? [*Optional line if doubling:* He went so fast I seem to have caught some of his clothing . . .]

Arthur   He's not one to sit still, that lad.

Anne   I'm so glad you came, Father. I couldn't go without saying goodbye. Thank you, for . . . you know.

Arthur   Whispers in the confessional, eh?

Da Souza   Your mind would boggle, Arthur. But it was my privilege. You're a remarkable young woman. A pain in the cassock at times, but never less than remarkable.

Anne   Does that mean I'm not excommunicated?

Da Souza   For now. Goodbye, Anne.

Anne   Wait! Father . . .

She steps away from **Arthur**, *closer to* **Da Souza** *to speak quietly.*

Anne   You told me to relinquish my guilt. So should you. There's no sin in you. You're the best grown-up I know.

Da Souza   Dear girl.

He sketches a blessing over her, then leaves.

Arthur   I'll pry some o' these secrets out of you, I swear, if there's another visit.

Anne   Oh, there will be. I've persuaded Mum to drive me up next half-term.

A car horn toots.

Though I'm still working on her patience.

Fiona *enters* [*if doubling, in a mix of* **Timmo** *and* **Da Souza***'s costumes, wheezing heavily*].

Anne   Mum! Is everything all right?

Fiona   [*Optional line if doubling:* It's been a bloody long show, little miss one role . . . Oh, all right. *Grudgingly adopts her character.*] It's just Prudie. She's a delight, of course, such a delight, but she has filled the car with cream buns because –

Anne/Arthur (*in unison*)   'You need a proper feed.'

Fiona   I've missed your lip, darling. I think we'll have plenty to talk about on the drive home, don't you?

Anne   I'm counting on it.

Fiona   Are you ready?

Anne   I think I am. [*Optional line if doubling:* There's no one left to say goodbye to.]

Fiona   [*Optional line if doubling:* Oh, thank God.]

Arthur   Bye, hinny.

Anne *and* **Fiona** *start to leave.*

Arthur   Lass. Divvent forget that Brigade badge. Makes you a member wherever you go in the world.

Anne   Don't worry, Arthur. That will stay with me forever.

Blackout.

Printed in the USA
CPSIA information can be obtained
at www.ICGtesting.com
LVHW020849171024
794056LV00002B/471